The curse
of the
Pharaohs

Yves NAUD

The curse of the of the Pharaohs

Volume 2

EDITIONS FERNI

TABLE OF CONTENTS

PART THREE

PART FOUR

PART FIVE

PART SIX

"To believe nothing or to believe everything are extreme positions which are equally futile."

Pierre Bayle

Dictionnaire historique et critique

PART ONE

TUTANKHAMEN –
THE LIFE AND DEATH
OF AN ILL-FATED PHARAOH

*"To pronounce the name of the dead
is to bring him back to life."*

Funerary inscription from Ancient Egypt

I N the Fall of 1922, the English archeologist Howard Carter started digging in the Valley of the Kings. What was he looking for? The tomb of Tutankhamen. The science of egyptology was just 100 years old, for it was in 1822 that Champollion had at last succeeded in deciphering the mysteries of hieroglyphics.

The tomb of Tutankhamen plundered by Horemheb

Among the many kings whose reigns have been documented by archeologists, that of Tutankhamen seems like a fleeting shadow. Few objects bear his name. The American Theodore Davis discovered a small number in 1906-1907. He thought that he had found the tomb of the king, plundered, like so many others, by grave-robbers. But other egyptologists disagreed: they thought that this was merely a secret chamber. In their opinion, the king's supporters had used it to store the objects rescued from his tomb, after it had been plundered by the Pharaoh Horemheb in attempt to erase the memory of his predecessors. In support of this theory, they cited the discovery of several monuments on which the name of the king had been obliterated and replaced by that of Horemheb.

The symbol of the curse of the Pharaohs

One thing was certain: in the section of the Valley of the Kings which Carter had surveyed were secret chambers and tombs dating from the XVIIIth Dynasty, to which Tutankhamen belonged.

This persuaded Carter to resume digging in the area, in particular between the tombs of Rameses IX and Rameses VI. This search would eventually enable him to unearth the burial chamber of Tutankhamen, with all its fabulous riches——the most spectacular archeological find of all time.

While Carter's team was carefully exploring the various chambers within the tomb, and cataloging its priceless treasures, the world's Press announced the discovery, linking the names of Lord Carnarvon, Carter and Tutankhamen in the same bold headlines. In the words of the funerary inscriptions of Ancient Egypt, Carter and Lord Carnarvon had just brought the Pharaoh back to life, by pronouncing his name . . .

The name of Tutankhamen lives on, synonymous with the riches of the Pharaohs, and as a symbol of the curse with which they pursue those who have troubled their repose.

However, the discovery of King Tutankhamen's tomb did not

solve all these problems. One question in particular remained to be answered: why had the Ancient Egyptians tried to blot out the memory of this king by removing his name from their monuments?

To attempt to answer this question, we must reconstruct, within the limits of our knowledge, the life of the boy king.

CHAPTER I

ATON REPLACES AMON:
THE RELIGIOUS REVOLUTION

"Thebes is the chief city, more powerful
than all the others... All cities are founded
in its name, because it is called The City.
All towns are watched over by Thebes. They
stand in its shadow and are glorified by it."

Papyrus of the XVIIIth Dynasty

THE reign of Tutankhamen was in an era as fascinating as it is confusing. Fascinating because it is marked by a full-scale religious revolution. Confusing since almost everything involving the actors in this sacred drama is shrouded in mystery.

Amon, the powerful god of Thebes

In the 16th century B.C., the Kings of Thebes drove out the Hyksos, invaders from Asia who had settled in the Nile Delta. Having liberated Egypt and placed it under their own rule, they extended the frontiers of their empire, which, in the 15th century B.C. under Thutmose III, stretched to the banks of the Euphrates.

At the moment when its kings liberated the country and thus built for themselves a vast empire, Thebes abandoned the local god Menthu in favor of Amon, chief of all the gods.

During the reign of Amenhotep III, Egypt reached the peak of its prosperity and power. Thebes became the glorious capital, the "chief city" of the empire. And the victories of Thebes were also the victories of its god, Amon, whose fortunes rose with those of the empire.

In order to establish their authority, the Pharaohs proclaimed themselves the "Sons of Amon." But this religious justification of their power was dangerous: against them, the priests of Amon, who guarded the temporal possessions of the god, were becoming daily more powerful. Amon, or his priests, possessed towns, villages, thousands of heads of cattle, vast lands, a fleet, not to mention huge quantities of gold and silver[1]. The administration of this

---

1.   The *Harris Papyrus* in the British Museum contains the following inventory of the amazing wealth of the priests of Amon: 82,000 vassals, 3,164 holy statues, 400,000 head of cattle, 1,500 square miles of wheatfields, 84 ships, 46 construction sites, 65 towns and villages, 7 of which were in Asia.

immense wealth required a huge staff, which was entirely outside the control of the Pharaoh.

With the power which this wealth brought, and their all-powerful religious influence, the high priests became increasingly involved with the process of government. An inscription found behind the statuette of the high priest Ptames proclaimed him "chief prophet of Amon, governor of the city of Thebes, vizier of Upper and Lower Egypt."

Political act or mystical ideal?

Amenhotep III, in the palace of Malgatta, to the southwest of Thebes, was only too well aware of the threat to his power which the growing domination of the priests represented. The religious reform which he intended to introduce—to replace Amon by another God—can be seen, at least in part, as a politically motivated act in order to strengthen his own power. But, at the same time, there was probably in the Pharaoh's plan the manifestation of a mystical ideal.

The people believed that "Amon the hidden one," in the image of a ghostly Pharaoh, saw everything without being seen. The priests cunningly exploited this divine power. But Amon did possess one visible attribute, Aton, which appeared every day in the form of Ra or Re, the Sun, and which provided a perfect image of a heavenly life-force upon which the whole earth depended. This was a notion which would be readily understood by the masses since it was visible both in its celestial form (the Sun itself) and in its human form (the Pharaoh, son of Ra or Re). Moreover, the new image would have the advantage of affecting all the peoples of the empire, who, in different forms, all worshipped the Sun.

To make the Sun the god of the empire would be to unite all men in a simple and universal faith.

Amenhotep III had great respect for the sun-gods, above all for the disk itself (the Eye of the Sun). He demonstrated this by building various temples, one of which—in Nubia—was called "Gem-Aton." His boat bore the name "Splendor of Aton," while his residence was described thus: "The House of Nibmatre, known as the Splendor of Aton."

Vengeance?

By dethroning Amon, the Pharaoh was able to pursue his own vengeance against the priests, who wanted to impose Thutmose as his successor. Thutmose, high-priest of Amon, was born of the Pharaoh's first marriage, before he married his beloved Teje, who gave him a son, Amenhotep IV. It was this son whom the Pharaoh wished to succeed to the throne. By disapproving of this choice, the priests of Thebes were condemning yet again the marriage of the Pharaoh and Teje. By marrying her, Amenhotep III had broken with the tradition which said that the king should take as his bride, and mother of the heir to the throne, the daughter of a Pharaoh.

Teje was of humble origin, at the very best she came from the minor aristocracy. Her parents Juja and Tuju, judging by their mummies, were probably Nubians. Religious officials in the cult of Amon in the provinces, they were showered with honors by the Pharaoh when they moved to Thebes. Juja, given the title "Divine Father," had—among his other duties—the rank of "Lieutenant General of Charioteers." As for Tuju, she was made governess of the harem of Amon.

It is true that, in order to compensate for this Nubian influence at court, the Pharaoh contracted other marriages with Asian princesses. Thus, in the tenth year of his reign, the arrival was announced of Gilhukhipa, daughter of Shutara, King of Nahrin. But these were purely political gestures: none of his other wives could conquer the place in the Pharaoh's affections held by the beloved Teje.

On the day of his marriage to her, Amenhotep III proclaimed to his empire the humble origins of his chosen queen. The priests of Amon would never forgive this challenge.

Political gesture? Mystical impulse? Vengeance? It is difficult to say for sure what was the prime motive behind the Pharaoh's dream of reform. Whatever it was, he was paving the way for a revolution which Amenhotep IV was destined to complete.

Amenhotep IV, the mystical Pharaoh

Although egyptologists are not in complete agreement, it is probable that Amenhotep IV became co-regent between the 27th and the 30th year of his father's reign.

It was about this time that Amenhotep IV married a girl whose name has been immortalised by her captivating beauty: Nefertiti.

Who was she? We cannot say for sure. Some have confused her with Taduhipa, daughter of Tushrata or Dushrata, King of Mitanni. But she did not arrive in Egypt until the 36th year of Amenhotep III's reign, by which time Nefertiti had already borne her husband four, possibly five, daughters. And the only known member of her family is her sister, Mutnejemet, who was not a princess.

One fact is certain: Nefertiti was not of royal descent, as some people have claimed. We know of her "wet nurse," a certain Ty, wife of Ay, who became "Divine Father" in his turn, and who would eventually be among the most fervent supporters of Amenhotep IV and his reforms. The young prince resented, like his father, the growing domination of the priests, and probably resolved to be rid of it. But he was, above all, a mystic, one of the greatest mystics of Antiquity, or so it is claimed.

He gave substance to his father's dream. He brought to completion the growing revolution, changing the god of the empire, transforming the rites used in the worship of the new deity, and creating a new capital city.

"Re, who appears in the shining disk of the Sun"

From the start of his own reign, Amenhotep IV planned to build at Karnak a temple dedicated to the rising sun, of which he would be the high-priest. This new deity would be "Re-Harkhti, who, on the horizon, rejoices in the name of Light of the Sun (Shu) and who appears in the shining disc of the Sun (Aton)."

The main ideas of the heretic Amenhotep IV are, for the most part, those of his father. He wished to bring people closer to their god by making him visible, to proclaim the equality of men and to free them from superstitious practices which prevented progress.

Amenhotep IV was encouraged by Nefertiti and Horemheb, the famous general who had secured peace in Asia. Of royal blood, and venerated as a sort of god, Horemheb saw, in the religious passion of the young prince an opportunity to maintain his own supremacy over the high priest of Amon.

But, needless to say, the plans of Amenhotep IV met with some opposition. Thebes was not the ideal place to carry out his reforms.

"Aton, my father ... I will build you a capital"

One morning, Amenhotep IV set forth from Thebes, riding in his small chariot, made of gold and silver, and drawn by two white horses. A fantastic journey had begun. The Pharaoh was going to choose the site of the city which would be dedicated to the new deity. A large tablet of red granite, standing halfway between Thebes and Memphis, on the Eastern bank of the Nile, recounts this fateful day:

"In the fourth year, on the thirteenth day of the fourth month of the second season, Amenhotep IV stood on this spot which will be the city of Aton. His Majesty returned to Thebes and sat upon his throne. 'Summon my own friends,' he said, 'the mighty, the handsome, the wise, the army commanders, and the nobles of the entire country.' And they all arrived and bowed down before His Majesty, who proclaimed: 'Aton has commanded me to build his city, to stand as an eternal monument to his glory. It was he who guided me to the place where I shall build the city of Aton in the land which is mine.'

His Majesty, raising his arms to heaven, exclaimed:

'To the East of the Nile, Aton, my father, in the place which you have chosen, I will build your city; all the peoples of the earth will journey there to worship you. I will build for you a temple shaded from the Sun, where Pharaoh's wife, Nefertiti, will come to worship you. There will stand the house of Aton, in all its splendor, to please you, Aton, my father."

Akhet-Aton, the city of the horizon of the Sun

Thousands of workmen set to work at once, and in a few years they had built the new capital city. Dedicated to Aton, it was called "Akhet-Aton," the City of the Horizon of the Sun. It corresponds to the present-day site of Tel el-Amarna.

Amenhotep IV erected fourteen impressive "stelae" (stone pillars bearing an inscription) to mark the boundaries of the city.

Five sanctuaries were planned, several palaces, as well as the tombs of the Pharaoh, Nefertiti and their eldest daughter Meritaton. To stress his determination to break with tradition, Amenhotep IV had these monuments constructed to the East of the city. For centuries, burial grounds had been constructed to the West of the Nile, where the Sun sets, and the dead are reborn after a slow and mysterious transformation.

And to underline this break with the old order of things, Amenhotep IV himself took the name of Ikhnaton (the servant of Aton according to some, the glory of Aton, according to others). He left Thebes with his courtiers and took up residence in his new capital.

The creed of Aton, an early example of monotheism

In this magnificent city, Ikhnaton built a sumptuous temple dedicated to the new deity, Aton, as well as a sanctuary dedicated to his ancestors. A papyrus describes the new religious capital as ''an enchanting city, delighting the eyes with its beauty, resembling a celestial vision.''

All the inscriptions found at Tel el-Amarna insist on the fact that Ikhnaton himself taught his people the wonders of the cult of Aton, which seems to have been an early form of monotheism, a century before the codification of Judaism under Moses.

Ikhnaton, according to the tablets engraved during his reign, taught that Aton was intangible, invisible but omnipresent. Both Mother and Father of mankind, Aton was revealed in the light of the Sun. He was not, however, the heavenly body itself, but the ''energy behind the Sun,'' the source of the life-force which comes to Earth from the heat of the Sun and which makes all things live and grow.

In addition to this, Aton did not have a human or animal form, unlike most Egyptian deities. No statue or likeness could be made of him. He was a purely spiritual entity, encompassing Goodness, Truth, Love and Happiness. Everything which is good on Earth is bathed in the spirit of Aton. Songs, music, love, laughter, health,

well-being, comfort, plenty, wine, flowers, the beauty of nature, the
song of birds, the murmur of the wind, the lapping of the water:
all this—in the words of an inscription of the time—is the handi-
work of Aton.

Ikhnaton and Mohammed, two politicals prophets

During the first five years of his reign, Ikhnaton showed himself
to be tolerant.

Conscious of the formidable power which the Theban priests still
retained, and also of the hostility which his religious revolution had
caused among the different classes of Egyptian society, reluctant as
they were to accept this extremely egalitarian form of monotheism
in which Egyptians, Nubians and Asians were urged to worship the
same gods with the same "fraternal devotion," Ikhnaton allowed
the traditional deities to survive, and left intact the temples and
shrines of the old religion. In this we can see the exceptional political judgment of this Pharaoh. The inspired prophet of a new religion, without doubt the first in the history of mankind, did not
ignore the practical problems caused by the foundation and development of the cult of Aton. He acted like Mohammed at Mecca and
Medina in a later century. The prophet of Islam would also try to
spread the word of Allah without offending the priests of the old
idolatrous polytheism of the desert tribes.

In that sense, Ikhnaton and Mohammed are the two greatest
"political prophets" of history.

The Pharaoh's missionaries massacred by the people

Ikhnaton's tolerance did not last beyond the fifth year of his reign.

Gradually, imperceptibly, he entered into open conflict with the priests of Thebes and the worshippers of Amon. His first act was to close the temples of this god, then to remove from the political scene the faithful of the old religion.

Its priests were removed from office and their possessions confiscated by the public exchequer.

In addition to this, Ikhnaton sent forth to all the provinces of his kingdom teams of missionaries, whose task was to teach the people about the new religion. These brave men did not hesitate to enter the temples to remove the symbols, names and titles of the old gods, who were doomed to disappear.

The inhabitants of certain provinces—particularly those which were far from the capital and therefore independent of central government—did not welcome the Pharaoh's messengers, who were, on at least one occasion, put to death by the inhabitants. In their devotion to their gods, they failed to grasp the metaphysical subtleties and speculations of their strange monarch.

The hymn to the one god of Ikhnaton

We know relatively little about the cult of Aton, which was destined to disappear along with its creator. But we can get some idea of it thanks to a document of great poetic beauty which has survived. It is a hymn composed by Ikhnaton in honor of the god Aton. It is one of the most evocative works in the whole of Ancient Egyptian literature. In its lyricism, its religious fervor and passionate intensity, the hymn of Ikhnaton anticipates the magnificence of Psalm 104, with its praise of the marvels of creation.

Here are a few extracts from this early religious manuscript:

> "Your beauty is without equal
> when you appear on the horizon,
> oh, living Aton, the source of all life!
> You give life to the child in its mother's womb,
> you feed it while it is there
> and keep it from crying.
> You give the breath of life to all that you create.
> When the child is born
> and leaves its mother's womb,
> you breathe so that he may speak
> and you minister to his needs.
> The chick inside the egg starts to talk
> because your breath is the air which gives him life.
> You give him strength to break out of the shell.
> As soon as he leaves the egg he starts to chirp;
> scarcely is he born that he starts to walk.
> Your works are infinite
> and full of mystery which the minds of men cannot fathom.
> You are the one God, without equal.

You created the Earth according to your plan
when you were still alone.
You created men, cattle and all creatures,
everything which walks on the Earth
or moves through the sky
or takes flight with wings,
foreign lands, Syria, Nubia
and the land of Egypt.
You have placed each man where he should be
and have provided for his needs.
To each man you give food
and the span of his life.
The tongues and words of man are different,
as are their characters and the color of their skin.
You created different races.
You are master of all,
You who labored for them,
oh, Aton, lord of the day
whose splendor is boundless!
You give life to all countries,
even the most remote;
your plans are perfect,
oh lord of all eternity!
You created the seasons of the year
so that all living things may grow.
Winter cools them
and Summer gives them fragrance.
You made the boundless sky

to display your power
and to see everything.
You are the one God."

Ikhnaton: Pharaoh, God and Pope

The spiritual revolution accomplished by Ikhnaton was accompanied by a complete change in public and private morality.

The inhabitants of both lands were urged to be "frugal, sincere, just and compassionate." Sorcerers were banished from the city, exposed and ridiculed. The virtuous and puritanical Egypt of Ikhnaton anticipates in some way the early years of the Christian Church.

The Pharaoh treated all his subjects alike. No privilege distinguished the high-born priest from the humblest "fellah." Certain courtiers, anxious to please the Pharaoh, left Thebes and traveled to Tel el-Amarna to pay homage to Ikhnaton. But he rejected them, preferring instead to reward genuine merit and virtue. He chose his aides from the lower classes. "I was a beggar outside the temple," wrote May, the new governor. "I began to worship Aton with all my heart and to love my neighbor, according to the commandments of my master, who then gave me towns and people to govern. Although I was not one of the Prince's entourage, I was made, by order of His Majesty, one of his confidants. It is His Majesty who elevates humble folk to the rank of princes."

At the same time, Ikhnaton tried to change the relationship between Egypt and the peoples under its rule. Carried along by his apostolic dream and his political vision, the Pharaoh saw beyond his frontiers Syrians, Hittites, Mitannians, Libyans and Tyrians linked in the worship of one universal god. He founded, in Nubia, the town of Geniaton—"the town which has found Aton"—and in Palestine, near Jerusalem, the town of Ikhutaton. These towns are an expression of the new Egyptian imperialism. At the same time Pharaoh, God and Pope, Ikhnaton created for the first time in history a sort of religious internationalism designed to give all nations a common ideal above and beyond purely political and commercial interests. Once again, the comparison between Ikhnaton and Mohammed is self-evident. The latter transformed Mecca into a spiritual capital where conquered peoples, all converted to Islam, would gather once a year to worship, on equal terms with the conquerors, before the black stone of the Kaba, and address the same fervent prayer to one great God. It is reminiscent too of medieval Christianity, with Rome as its focal point, where the power of the Church, with its monasteries open to the lower classes, held sway over kings and nations.

The death of Ikhnaton

But Ikhnaton did not possess the tremendous energy which characterized the Moslem prophet or the great monks of the Middle Ages, and his dream soon came face to face with harsh reality.

While the young ruler is preaching love, peace and joy, revolts broke out in almost every part of the empire. General Horemheb, who merely paid lip service to the pacifism of his master, was for crushing the rebels; but Ikhnaton, increasingly obsessed with his mystic dream, forbade him to fight. On the subject of the troubles which were to lead to the eventual disappearance of the Atonist heresy, we possess one amazing document, the famous *Letters of Tel el-Amarna*. These terra-cotta tablets covered in cuneiform script contain the dispatches, often couched in desperate terms, sent to the Pharaoh by his loyal subjects. They allow us to reconstruct the dramatic events which marked the break-up of the Empire of the Pharaos.

The loyal citizens of Tunip, a Syrian city threatened by the rebels, implored Ikhnaton to send help:

"Tunip, your city, weeps, and its tears flow, for there is no hope for us. For years we have sent messengers to our Master, the King of Egypt, but we have received no reply, not a single word..."

Abdkhiba, his loyal vassal, King of Jerusalem, asked in vain for reinforcements to crush sedition and defend his territory: "Let the King watch over the land and send troops, because, if they do not arrive this year, the whole territory of the King and Master will be lost." And he added a post-script, probably intended for one of the Pharaoh's courtiers: "Explain this clearly to the King—the whole country is heading for disaster!"

It was amid this atmosphere of decline, revolt and defeat that Ikhnaton died, to be succeeded by a ten-year-old boy, Tutankhaton.

Ikhnaton (1375 to 1354 B.C.), the world's first monotheistic sovereign, and his wife Nefertiti. He abandoned Thebes for El-Amarna: "Aton (the sun) has commanded me to erect this city as an eternal monument to his glory." *Musée du Louvre, Giraudon.*

Chapter II

THE MYSTERIOUS LINEAGE
OF TUTANKHATON

"You rise in splendor on the horizon
Oh Aton, creator of all life!
When you appear you fill the Earth with your beauty.
You are magical, divine, when you shine upon the Earth.
Your rays envelope the whole of your creation.
You are far away, but your light is on Earth..."

Hymn to Aton, discovered in the tomb of Ay

THE accession of Tutankhaton to the throne of Egypt at the age of ten remains an enigma.

What was the lineage of this young sovereign which gave him the right to succeed Ikhnaton?

Scholars can only guess... Were his parents Amenhotep III and Teje? Or was he the offspring of Amenhotep III and a secondary wife of whom we know nothing? Or was he the child of a son, (whose existence has yet to be demonstrated), of Ty and Ay, (the foster parents of Nefertiti) and a daughter of Amenhotep III and Teje? Or even the son of Ikhnaton himself?

A King shrouded in mystery since birth

Of all these theories let us consider the one which sees Tutankhaton as the son of Amenhotep III and Teje. In support of what is merely a hypothesis—but perhaps the most credible of all—we must consider the objects found in his tomb and the remnants of monuments erected during his reign.

On a sacred lion in the temple of Soleb, Tutankhaton calls Amenhotep III his "father," and several objects in his tomb seem to substantiate this. The best example of this is a small gold statue of Amenhotep III, crouching in the same position as the child of the Sun himself, thus indicating that the King perpetuated himself in his son, flesh of his flesh. In a small sarcophagus next to the one containing this statuette is a lock of hair from Queen Teje. Among the other objects which recall the king's parents is an alabaster pitcher bearing the name of Amenhotep III.

We should also mention the likeness of the features, the resemblance of the shape of the skull of Tutankhaton and of the body first said to be that of Ikhnaton then that of Smenkhare, who was briefly Tutankhaton's co-regent. Such similarities suggest that the young king was the brother of either. Indeed, it seems likely that Ikhnaton and Smenkhare were brothers, or, at least, half-brothers.

Lastly, the face of Tutankhaton bears a striking resemblance to that of Queen Teje.

As for the name Tutankhaton itself—which was later to be changed to Tutankhamen—it proves that the boy, like his sister born two or three years earlier, was consecrated to the Sun-God, Aton.

But the exact meaning of the name is far from clear. Some scholars say that Tutankhaton means "Aton, whose life is full of grace"; others take it to mean "Powerful is the life of Aton"; while others read it as "the living image of Aton." A fourth possibility is: "All life is in the hands of Aton." Linguists and philosophers have so far not reached agreement on this point.

Like a little scribe

Nor do we know for sure the birthplace of Tutankhaton. Was it Thebes or Tel el-Amarna? There is no document to provide the answer, but one or two inscriptions offer us clues suggesting that he spent part of his childhood in either of these rivaling cities, which both were to leave their mark on him.

In ancient Egypt the education of the children began at an early age.

It is likely that from the age of four, Tutankhaton attended the Palace School. There, he would have mixed with the children of the nobility as well as the foreign princes of the "kep."

What was the "kep"? It is difficult to define it closely. It was most likely a kind of military academy created for the young

Nubian princes brought to Egypt as a guarantee of their father's loyalty to the Pharaoh. They were brought up with the royal children and treated with great respect. Once their schooling was over, they went back to Nubia to assist the Viceroy, or they served as officers in the Pharaoh's army.

In the mornings, Tutankhaton and his young friends would begin the study of hieroglyphics. Then they would do some grammar, some mental arithmetic and hieratic script, which was reserved for sacred texts. Next they would learn the language of literature and how to translate from foreign languages.

Tutankhaton would have written upon papyrus, made from the fibre of reeds—a material too precious to be used by children of lower rank. They would have done their assignments on pieces of broken pottery or pieces of rock.

Like a small scribe, Tutankhaton would have had a small palette—probably of ivory—at the top of which were two hollows to contain the blocks of color (black and red). In the center, in a small hole, were the small reeds used for writing, with their tips in the form of paintbrushes. There was also a small piece of sandstone to erase mistakes and a smoother to polish the surface of the papyrus after using the eraser.

The afternoons were devoted to physical education, in particular wrestling and swimming.

"One profitable day at school is for all time"

Once these elementary studies had been completed, young Tutankhaton learned the art of writing, under the watchful eye of the most capable tutors. They would have reminded him of the immense advantage he would enjoy by becoming a scholar. His education would make him exceptional. "One profitable day at school is for all time..." they told him. "He who uses the palette is far above those who wield the oar."

This academic education was accompanied by Tutankhaton's initiation into the art of hunting. Although his health was not good, his instructors took him off to the desert in pursuit of gazelle and antelope. They showed him how to use a bow, to hurl a javelin and to wield a dagger—weapons reserved for members of the royal household.

For relaxation, the young Prince walked his dogs through the Palace gardens. He played for hours with a sort of flint toy which gave off sparks. This he must have enjoyed, since it was found among the objects in his tomb.

"My sister arrives and my heart swells..."

The parents of the young Tutankhaton often traveled to Tel el-Amarna. His brother Ikhnaton had built a palace for Amenhotep III and Teje, his favorite wife. It was called "Splendor of Aton" and stood at the heart of the new religious capital. The steward of Queen Teje has recorded for posterity in the chapel of his tomb one of their visits to Amarna. We see Ikhnaton and his wife Nefertiti seated side by side to receive homage from their daughters, while Teje sits opposite her husband.

For Tutankhaton, the time spent at Amarna must have been full of happiness and relaxation. We can see him, splashing in the water with his nieces during the morning bath. After drinking milk from alabaster bowls, lying face down on the ground covered with lapis-lazuli powder, the children would play the "Game of the Serpent"—forerunner of the game of the goose—moving the ivory pieces with their young, nimble fingers.

Then it would be time to eat. While the children ate their food with fine golden needles, they listened to songs like this one, discovered on a papyrus:

"My sister arrives and my heart swells. I open my arms to embrace her and my heart beats faster in my breast."

After the singers, the dwarfs would appear, with their irresistible antics. Last would come the acrobats with their graceful pirouettes.

The immortal maxims of the scribe Ani

After the meal, the children's tutors would give them a lesson based on the philosophical maxims of the scribe Ani, of which the Bulaq papyrus provides a sample:

"Think always of your mother. May you never give her cause for reproach, or make her pray to god in desperation on your account."

After philosophy would come history. The tutor would describe the incredible adventures of the Barons of Elephantine who had

brought back from far-off Libya the dwarfs to entertain the Pharaoh.
The children were enthralled by the exploits of General Tuti, and
when the tutor related how—to capture the town of Joppe—Tuti
smuggled in soldiers hidden in huge earthenware pitchers, they
burst out laughing and clapped their hands.

This was how Tutankhaton spent his childhood, which we have
been able to reconstruct thanks to the many illustrations and writings found in his tomb.

A frail child in a world of intrigues

Then came the death of Ikhnaton.

Intrigues surrounded Tutankhaton, who had just reached the tender age of ten.

In the City of the Sun, relatives and courtiers alike defied openly
any challenge to the Atonist revolution. It is true that many of them
owed their position and wealth to the rise of Aton.

For their part, the priests of Amon hoped that this frail child
would not stand in the way of the restoration of their privileges and
the revival of the cult of Amon.

But this was to reckon without Ay, the "Divine Father," husband
to the wet nurse of Nefertiti, who well understood what the priests
were plotting. He held one trump card, though. He knew that the
priests needed the support of the army to prevent the erosion of
the nation's frontiers. For he was the Lieutenant General of the
Charioteers—a corps composed of the highest aristocracy—and
thus held sway over the officers.

Ay is not merely sly-faced, he has also the mentality of a conspirator; he was happy only in the midst of intrigue. Horemheb, who—like Ay—coveted the throne, was a man of far greater stature. This brilliant military chief, who had won great fame in Asia, was adept at reconciling his own interests with those of the nation. An astute politician, and, above all, an opportunist, he would not hesitate to change his religion, or rally to another master, to achieve his ambition.

It is likely, that the "Divine Father" had a tacit agreement with Horemheb to firm, and also control, the power of the boy prince.

Tutankhaton was to reign as long as Ay and Horemheb were in power.

"The Eternal Hour"

To secure the position of the young Tutankhaton, he was married to Ankhesenpaaten, also quite young, and whose divine lineage had been established just shortly before that through a marriage with Ikhnaton, her husband's father.

After the ceremony, the young couple found themselves alone at dusk, the "eternal hour" which artists have immortalized on several objects found in the king's tomb[1].

Tutankhaton is seated on a stool with feet in the shape of a lion's paw. He wears around his waist a fine pleated muslin gar-

---

1.   Scenes depicted on the golden *naos*, the back of the throne, and on a perfume jar.

ment. On his bare feet are gold sandals. With his bracelet-covered arm he anoints the young queen's head with precious perfumes. Kneeling on a cushion, she wears a pleated robe, the upper part of which is covered by a breast-plate set with precious stones. She stands up, and takes a richly decorated fan which she waves gently before the young king. Following tradition, she then anoints him with fragrant oils and says:

"Oh, artemisia[1] of my brother, in whose presence I feel great, I am your favorite sister and I will follow you, as I did through the field which I planted with flowers. . . . where flow the lovely streams which I have created with my own hand to cool me in the north wind; this delightful place where I can walk with you, hand in hand, my heart full of joy for we are walking together."

Then, locked in a tender embrace, the young couple go toward the ebony beds which stand in the shadow at the far end of the room.

---

1. A perennial plant with a powerful scent, whose different varieties act like appetizers, digestives, stimulants or tonics.

CHAPTER III

THE KING'S APPRENTICESHIP

*"Send me ten times more gold than my brothers
received; for I was on the best of terms
with your father Amenhotep III."*

Letter from Dushratta, King of
Mitanni, to Ikhnaton

WITH the ascension of Tutankhaton, we are plunged
once more into the realms of speculation. Egyptologists do agree on one point, however; the boy king
who was about ten when crowned, reigned for just nine years. But
it is not easy to fit his reign into any chronology. Some scholars
place it between 1369 and 1360 B.C.; others between 1357 and
1350 B.C.; but more plausible is the theory which places it
between 1352 and 1344 B.C. When Ikhnaton died, after a twenty-

year reign starting in 1372 B.C., the young prince found himself in
the City of the Sun, the capital of the new heresy.

The citizens wondered as to who would win over the mind of
the boy king—the followers of Aton, or those of Amon.

"I will rebuild what has been ruined"

What arguments did the priests of Amon use to influence the
king? Nobody knows... Whatever they were, Tutankhaton returned
to Thebes.

Horemheb, the opportunist, backed down. Egypt had taken the
wrong course, he conceded in private. It was now time to return to
tradition, to restore the old capital to its glory, with its gods and its
priesthood.

Horemheb—so he claimed—had to deal with more pressing
problems. He had to try to reverse the worsening situation in Asia.

In reality, his departure offered him an ideal opportunity not to
have to denounce in public the heresy to which he had rallied. He
hoped that when he returned, all this would have been forgotten.

He gets Ay to take the young king back to the old deserted
capital. And to make sure of this, the general made the people
and the army join with the priests to demand the prince's return to
Thebes.

But before he was allowed to revert to the old religion, the
priests demanded of him to solemnly denounce the heresy. Tutankhaton gave in and issued the decree which was later to be
engraved on the granite stone of Karnak:

"I shall rebuild the eternal monuments which have been ruined.
I shall banish the lie from the Two Lands and I shall restore the
Truth."

"I, herewith, crown you King of the North and King of the South"

The coronation of the boy king was to mark the restoration of
the cult of Amon. Therefore, it was decided that the ceremony will
take place at Karnak, where Amenhotep IV, before he became the
heretic king, had been crowned.

Bareheaded, merely dressed in a loincloth, and escorted by the
high dignitaries, Tutankhaton advanced across the first courtyard
where the obelisks of Thutmose I and Thutmose III rose into the
sky.

The priests who received him had donned their animal masks
whose roles they were to enact.

Holy water was poured over him, and now he was ready to
appear before the gods. The mantle of the Pharaohs was placed on
his shoulders, the regal symbols were offered to him: the hook, the
whip and the scepter. The golden beard of the gods was affixed to
his chin, an honor reserved solely for the kings and the gods. The
priests impersonating Horus and Seth placed on his head the white
crown of Lower Egypt and the red crown of Upper Egypt, which
together constituted the *Pschent*.

"I, hereby, bestow upon you the dignity of King of the North,"
said the priest wearing the mask of Horus.

"I, hereby, bestow upon you the dignity of King of the South," added the priest wearing the mask of Seth.

And now he was given his royal name, Nebkeprure.

And the high priest continued:

"Oh my son, Lord of the Crowns, I bind together the lotus and the papyrus to place the Two Lands under your dominion forever and also the entire country from the plains to the mountains for you are endowed with the voice of creation."

The king then entered the holiest of the holy of the temple to pray before the *naos*—dwelling place of the gods.

The king pressed the statue of Osiris to his breast to receive the "fluid of life." He then adorned the statue with jewels before putting it back in place.

Before withdrawing, the king made the traditional offering and chanted a hymn of praise to the god.

The ceremony was over now. The child had become Pharaoh, and had taken the name of Tutankhamen.

One hundred oxen and female slaves

After the coronation, the king returned to the City of the Sun, where he remained for a time with the consent of the Theban priests. It was probably around the fourth year of his reign that he began to reside permanently in Thebes.

Once the move had been decided, Tutankhamen, with the help of his aides, selected the archives which he would take with him to Thebes. Assisted by the chief archivist, Ra-Api, the Keeper of the

Seal, Tetu-Nu, and the Babylonian scribe, Shamas-Niki, the king chose the clay tablets which would be transferred to the new capital.

His ancestors, the Pharaohs, in their wisdom, had abandoned hieroglyphics in favor of cuneiform script, which was used for seven or eight Asiatic languages. Papyri and reed brushes were replaced by clay tablets and nails that were embedded in them, to form the characters.

As he read the small tablets, the king discovered that the main aim of the Pharaohs' foreign policy had always been to reinforce the Eastern frontiers of the empire.

In twenty years, the Thutmose Pharaohs had conquered the lands beyond the isthmus of Suez: Syria, Phoenicia, Babylonia, Assyria and Mitanni, kingdoms of the Euphrates and the Taurus.

His father, Amenhotep III, had laid down a flexible but firm policy attuned to each of these countries.

The king learned also to distinguish between vassals and allies among the conquered people. The former were under the direct rule of the Pharaoh, but the governors of the conquered cities were chosen from among the natives. They were the *kazani*, whose loyalty is mirrored in the reports which they sent the Pharaoh:

"I am the King's servant, his dog," wrote one.

"I, your servant, the dust under your feet, I lie down before the King and Master and send him one hundred oxen and female slaves," wrote another.

An effective yet inexpensive gesture

His aides explained to Tutankhamen how these countries were governed so effectively at such little cost.

Egyptian officials were few in number, for the *kazani* ruled in the name of the Pharaoh. There was no policy of colonialist brutality. The natives kept their kings, their gods and their laws. The tribute which they paid the Pharaoh was a fair exchange for the peace and prosperity which they enjoyed under Egypt's rule.

Moreover, Egypt knew how to make sure of their loyalty. Young native princes, like those of Nubia, were taken to Egypt, where they were little more than hostages. Whenever a throne fell vacant, it was from their ranks that the Pharaoh himself chose the one likely to be the most loyal successor. If the choice turned out to be a poor one, and the newly designated king showed signs of rebelliousness, repression was swift and ruthless. Men such as Horemheb saw to that.

"Divide and rule"—one of the principles of Egyptian diplomacy

Allied nations, explained the aides, were those too powerful to be conquered by Egypt.

The sovereigns of these nations were on equal terms with the Pharaoh. To prove the point, the chief-archivist showed Tutankhamen a small tablet which bore the inscription:

"I, King of Alasia, salute you my brother!"

The high priests of Amon were a serious threat to the power of the Pharaoh. Amenophis IV (XVIIth dynasty 1372 to 1354 B.C), encouraged by his wife, Nefertiti, replaced the cult of Amon by that of Aton. The latter is shining on the King and the Queen who are both holding the symbol of life in their hands (ankh). *The Cairo Museum, Editions Arthaud.*

It was in this familiar fashion that the allied kings addressed the Pharaoh.

The young king also discovered that the best way of cementing an alliance was by marriage.

After an unsuccessful approach to the King of Babylon, the Pharaohs turned towards the King of Mitanni. The geographical location of this country—to the East of the Euphrates—made it an ideal buttress, protecting the eastern flank of Egypt from the kingdom of the warlike Hittites, who occupy Anatolia. For his part, the King of Mitanni needed Egypt's support to defend himself against the Assyrians and the Hittites. An alliance was therefore of mutual advantage, and it grew closer during the reign of Amenhotep III.

Reading the small clay tablets, the King realizes how flexible diplomacy has to be. He also learns that the principle of "divide and rule" produces goods results.

But, with the countries of the south there was no need for such diplomatic subtleties. Force alone was enough. The Thutmoses had made Nubia a dominion. The young king therefore appointed a Viceroy to ensure his hold over these territories, for they provided in great quantity the gold upon which Egypt depended for its economy, its alliances with the greedy Asian kings and for the luxury goods which Egypt's craftsmen fashioned with such great art.

It was underdeveloped Africa which provided the raw materials for Egypt's industry.

Tutankhamon has the tablets, on which the treaties of alliance are recorded, gathered. They will be good models for the future. He understands how precious they are because of the detailed information they contain, especially for Egypt's economy. He learns how the countries of Asia provide the raw material which Egypt needs: timber, metals, etc. At the same time, Asia was also the main outlet for the finished products made by Egypt's craftsmen.

To the young Tutankhamen, these communications between kings must have looked like tough transactions between brokers. "Your envoy," complains Amenhotep II to the King of Alazia, "has brought twenty *mines* of impure gold, which, when melted down barely yields five *mines* of pure gold."

Tutankhamen also realizes that the prosperity of his country depends mainly on the work of its craftsmen and artists. And the treaties endeavor to safeguard this. They contain a clause of extradition should any artisan be tempted to exercise his craft abroad.

The seafarers of Tyr and Byblos and the Pharaoh's harem

The young ruler entered the second chamber of the archives, which contained more tablets than the first. They represented a complete record of the maritime policies of the Pharaohs.

Tutankhamen knew of the importance of his fleet, greatly feared by all his neighbors. It was composed of long, narrow boats with a single sail. Their stern was decorated with a lotus flower; their prow bore an animal's head, which, in time of war was replaced by a huge metal spike to strike terror in the hearts of the enemy. The power of the Egyptian fleet is summed up by the inscription of

Medinet-Abu: "I made their ships capsize, and their riches were swallowed by the sea."

The fleet had several functions: it was a war machine of the highest efficiency; but it was also a first class merchant marine.

The hardy seafarers of Tyr and Byblos, fearing the power of Egypt, placed themselves under the Pharaoh's protection. They paid him a substantial tirbute in exchange for the right to carry on their trade without any trouble.

The Pharaoh was, for good reason, indulgent with these seafarers. Shrewd businessmen, they provided most of the women for his harem.

The Asians' love of gold and gifts

Leaving the royal archives, the Pharaoh moved on to the office of the translators.

He bent over their desks to observe them as they worked. In front of them was the dictionary compiled "by order of His Majesty." Opposite each word or phrase in cuneiform script are three columns: in the first was the ideogram, in the second, a translation into Semitico-Babylonian—a language common to most of the Asian Empire—and, in the third, the pronunciation in Sumerian or Babylonian. The Pharaoh must have admired this system, but he had to move on quickly to the dispatching room.

Here were received all the complaints from the people of the Empire, requests for military aid, disputes to be settled, etc.

By far the most numerous were the tablets referring to disputes, mostly family ones. How many quarrels and quibblings were recorded there!

The Asian fathers-in-law of the Pharaohs demanded gold, more gold and lots of other gifts in exchange for the dowries they had given their daughters.

Even more problems were caused by the ascension of a new Pharaoh. Thus the Hittite King wrote to Ikhnaton after the death of his father: "Continue to grant us the same amount of gold as did your father, but first send us what is due."

"The eyes and ears of the King"

Sickened by the endless greed recorded on these tablets, Tutankhamen proceeded to the room containing the correspondence of the Pharaohs with their envoys.

These tablets recorded the often difficult negotiations leading to the marriages between the Pharaohs and eastern princesses.

Other tablets contained the envoys' reports to the Pharaoh. These diplomats took up residence in allied nations or conquered territories and supplied the Pharaoh with information about events there. They returned to Egypt only every seven years.

Tutankhamen supervised the preparation of one last big bundle of tablets—the dispatches from the royal informers (razibu). They occupied a lower rank in the diplomatic service, but their role was nonetheless vital. They provide information on a whole range of matters, but were concerned above all with poorly known territories, which they explored on the king's behalf. From their reports, the young monarch would glean valuable information to help him avoid mistakes in foreign policy or to locate new quarries and gold mines.

The mission of these agents was often a dangerous one. Their dispatches make this clear. But the new king would reward them handsomely.

Tutankhamen was by now quite exhausted. The first bundles of tablets were ready now. The following day, a long train of mules will carry them to Thebes.

CHAPTER IV

THE "GREAT OFFICE"

"His Majesty erected monuments to all the gods...
He rebuilt their shrines as eternal monuments...
He created more than had existed since the time
of Re and his ancestors..."

Extracts from the decree carved on the big
stele of Tutankhamen at Karnak

THE day after this inspection of the archives, the king, his court, his officials and his harem left the city of the Sun for Thebes.

This departure closed a chapter in the history of Egypt which had opened fifteen years earlier with the exodus of an enthusiastic crowd towards the new capital, destined to be the symbol of a new world of brotherhood and love.

But the dream——as we have seen——did not last. The City of the Sun would soon be no more than a ghost town, haunted only by a handful of artists and a few devotees of Aton who would die there in solitude.

It was in Thebes, once again capital of the empire, that Tutankhamen would carry out his duties as king——the "great office," as the Egyptians call it.

The great many papyri and paintings of this era provide a glimpse of the Pharaoh in this role.

The raids of Pharaoh's "special commandos"

When he reached Thebes, where did Tutankhamen take up residence?

In all probability in the palace which Amenhotep III built for Teje on the left bank of the Nile. There, behind the brick ramparts, and set amid gardens, stood the huge royal edifice which the Egyptians called "the double palace."

After crossing the courtyard, you went through a maze of corridors to reach the ceremonial chambers. The massive doors, made of rare woods and precious metals, opened onto huge rooms lined with tall, warmly colored columns. The whitewashed walls were covered with exquisite frescoes, and the floors shone with colorful mosaics.

Beyond the ceremonial chambers were the royal apartments, decorated with arabesques and flower designs, and separated by small ornamental gardens whose fountains murmured gently.

From the terrace, Tutankhamen could see Thebes. Along the opposite bank of the river, the huge city stretched for over thirty miles. Amid the temples and the red brick houses proudly stood, behind their crenelated walls, some twenty, gleamingly white buildings: the ministries and storehouses of the Pharaoh. They were all built on the same design. Inside the walls, two avenues, lined with sycamore and tamarisk trees, crossed at right angles, marking the boundaries of four separate blocks.

The most important was that of the king's own household. It contained all the supplies, clothing and other objects needed by the Pharaoh and his court.

Among the other ministries was, for example, the "Per-Hazu," which dealt with fabrics, jewels and wine; the "Per-Hedu," which received cattle, the "Per-Nubu," which stored grain; and the "Per-Hudu," which was an armory containing the arrows, spears, javelins and shields which were distributed each month, under the presidency of Tutankhamen, to the troops being sent off to rebel areas, and to the "special commandos" ordered on behalf of the Pharaoh to carry out profitable raids in enemy territory to boost the royal treasury.

Three or four hundred women in the Pharaoh's harem

The royal residence housed many people whose life was governed by a strict and complex code of conduct.

The *Hood Papyrus* tells us, for example, that certain people were allowed to wear sandals in the Palace, while others had to remove them. Some were allowed to kiss the sovereign's feet, others his knees. People of the highest rank were permitted to wear a panther skin over their shoulders.

The hierarchy was just as complex. There were the "special friends" or counselors; the "custodians of the secret of the royal household," who watched over the treasury; and the "custodians of the secret of the royal word," who decided who could be admitted to the great courtyard when the king addressed his subjects from the balcony.

Among the many dignitaries and officials who hovered round the king, the most important were the "custodians of heaven" *(Rhi-habi)*. Priests, sorcerers and soothsayers, they had the power to summon spirits, to deliver incantations and to interpret dreams.

The king was attended to by many servants. The representatives of twenty crafts were busy with Tutankhamen's beauty care. There were the king's wigmakers, the manicurists, the creators of oils and perfumes to rub the king's body, and many others beside.

Those in charge of the royal jewels and the royal wardrobe were equally numerous.

Each day, hordes of launderers would solemnly descend towards the river, conscious of the great importance of their task. To them, cleanliness and religious purity were closely interrelated.

There were also countless servants and slaves of all descriptions. And, if we include the many members of the harem, it would be no exaggeration to say that the royal palace was a city within a city.

The harem was a world apart. There were three or four hundred women, among whom were the eastern princesses with their own impressive retinue of servants, musicians, dancers and clowns. There was also a huge staff needed to supervise and tend to the needs of the harem.

"Beware of the alien woman—she is like deep and boundless waters"

In the intense heat of the afternoon, the Pharaoh would often relax in the cool of the vast apartments of the harem, with their multi-colored pillars reflected in the waters of the pools and fountains.

When Tutankhamen entered, a swarm of beautiful, naked *palla-cides* would gather round him, their huge eyes made up with *kohol* and their nails painted scarlet. These *pallacides* (the name given to them by Diodoros of Sicily, the Greek historian) were like the young women who devoted themselves to the cult of the gods—notably Amon—and who were chosen from among the most beautiful daughters of the Theban aristocracy. One would proffer a slice of iced melon to quench the Pharaoh's thirst, another would hold a fragrant lotus blossom close to his face, while others would produce a small table upon which they would place a checkerboard.

The young king, now completely at his ease, would forget for a moment the burden of his office and the intrigues of his courtiers.

When evening came, the king would go to an upper floor composed of small rooms with, at one end, an alcove containing a couch covered with cushions. It was time for the king to pay his respects to the foreign princesses. But, at this point, Tutankhamen would hesitate, and not just because of his natural shyness. The harem had always been a place of base and often tragic intrigue. Tutankhamen was aware of this, and no doubt recalled the maxims of Ani which his tutor had taught him: "Beware of the alien woman; she is like deep and boundless waters."

The "Divine Father" and "Supreme Confidant"

These few hours spent in the "house of love" (the harem) were but a brief respite for this frail youth, already worn out by the crushing burden of kingship.

Did he actually reign? It rather seems that Ay and Horemheb dictated the guiding lines of the young king's policies. Commander-in-chief of Charioteers, Ay—the Divine Father—was also Lord of the Seal, or Secretary of the Treasury. Was he also Vizier of the South? Possibly; but we cannot be sure. He held full authority over the Pharaoh, openly and unrivaled. This is evident from his incredible audacity in having his likeness displayed in the place usually reserved for Amon. This is how he appears on a fragment of gold discovered in the cache unearthed by Davis in 1906 and which he took to be the tomb of Tutankhamen.

As for Horemheb, who had just stabilized the situation in the turbulent provinces of the empire, he exerted considerable influence at court if we take into account the many titles which he boasts to have received from the king: "Deputy to the King in all lands" or, in other words, vice-regent; "Chief of the Administration, by command of the King"; also the "King's own favorite scribe," "Chief Steward" and "Supreme Confidant of the King."

If this abundance of titles reveals the Orientals' love of grandeur, it also betrays the influence of Horemheb over the young ruler, and perhaps also over Ay, who was already old. One wonders whether he was not in fact a real dictator. Did he not call himself "The greatest of the great, the mightiest of the mighty, the lord of the people?"

No written law restricts the power of the Pharaoh

Under the watchful eye of these two eminences, Tutankhamen pursues the "democratic" policies of his predecessors. In the provinces, the nobility constituted an assembly, or *quenbet*, where they freely discussed the Pharaoh's decisions. The delegates appointed by the various *quenbets* formed a kind of parliament. Tutankhamen consulted its members frequently and took their opinions into consideration.

Like his predecessors, Tutankhamen delegated his authority to three viziers. One lived in Memphis, and governed Lower Egypt. The second, who bore the title "Royal Prince of Kush," was viceroy of Nubia. The third, and most important, was the Grand Vizier, who resided in Thebes and exercised authority over the capital and Upper Egypt. He was also the Secretary of the Interior, Secretary of Defense, Attorney General and Secretary of Commerce.

The tasks of this Grand Vizier covered even quite practical aspects which he dealt with in person. It was not unusual to see him supervising tree-felling in the palace gardens or inspecting the supplies of drinking water.

The Pharaoh had always to show himself to be just. He was often told to remember the lesson taught by the great Thutmose to his vizier, Rekh-mara: "Avoid what was said of the vizier Kheti, that he sided with his relatives against strangers. That is not justice. What God abhors is to favor one side over the other."

This quest for justice tempered the King's absolute authority, for there was no written law which limited his power.

"The bandits of Shumardata have cut off the feet of my men"

The first task which awaited the monarch each day was to listen to the grievances of his subjects.

In the great hall on the ground floor of the Palace, there is gathered a motley crowd who wished to have an audience with their king. There were the Pharaoh's own envoys, returning from their posts abroad, foreign ambassadors bearing gifts and messages, generals back from distant campaigns, courtiers and the most humble folk.

Ay would lead them, one by one, into the audience chamber. Tutankhamen, wearing the royal diadem and holding the symbols of office, sat motionless beneath a canopy.

As soon as he had entered the chamber the person seeking audience would prostrate himself until the Pharaoh ordered him to rise. He would then deliver a speech of homage, praising at length——as was customary——the greatness of the King and of Egypt.

Let us imagine one of the Pharaoh's envoys, who has come to

report the failure of his mission. His face betraying fear and desperation, his voice trembling, he confesses his misfortune:

"My agents met a violent death in Palestine. The bandits of Shumardata cut off their feet and fingers... and stole all the gold bars which I was carrying on Your Majesty's behalf to your good brother, the King of Babylon. You can make an investigation—we are not the robbers..."

Grievances and reports would follow one another. Tutankhamen would listen in silence, impassive. His face would betray no emotion.

Consulting the god Amon—a pretense which fooled nobody

After the audience was over Tutankhamen would go, as he did every day, to Karnak. He would consult the gods on all the problems he had heard. Should he punish the envoy whose mission had failed? What answer should he give the ambassador of the Prince of Megiddo, who was seeking military aid from Egypt to combat the forces of the warlike Akitisu? Should he take action against the Governor of Thebes, the director of Public Works? Tutankhamen knows only too well that all his officials, from the Governors down to the scribes who paid out the wages, took their cut off the workers' wages. Under these circumstances it was no wonder that the men building the temple of Konsu had gone on strike.

The shortened rations of wheat, millet and oil which they were given at the beginning of the month could not possibly last them until the next month, even if the men ate very little.

Wearing his loincloth of pleated linen and the white miter of Lower Egypt, Tutankhamen would leave the Palace in his small chariot. Runners preceded him to make the crowds that clogged the streets give way. The King was escorted by some thirty soldiers.

After he had arrived at the temple, Tutankhamen would make his way through the many chambers, heavy with the smell of incense, until he reached the shrine. There the High Priest would open the doors of the *naos* and remove a jointed wooden statue of Amon. He would burn some incense and hold in front of the god two papyrus scrolls. The first called for an investigation into the dealings of the Governor of Thebes; the second said that such an investigation was unnecessary. The priest invoked Amon: "Thou shalt judge, Oh Master!"

The jointed arm of Amon this time chose the papyrus demanding an investigation. Thebes would have a new governor. Amon—that is, the High Priest—had spoken.

Then the King himself questioned the god. He wanted to send men to the lands of Punt in search of new treasures[1].

---

1.   Where exactly were these strange lands? Were they real or mythical? In the first volume of the excellent *Histoire générale de l'Afrique* (François Beauval, 1971), we read: "These countries remain legendary, although some authors have situated them in the extreme southeastern part of Egypt near Eritrea or the Somali Coast. Their inhabitants are supposed to have lived in huts set on stilts beside the rivers and lakes. They traded with the few travelers who chanced to come to this mysterious country in gold, ivory, make-ups, ebony, turpentine and incense. The site of Cape Hafun, 100 miles to the south of Cape Guardafui, and the Bay of Hafun which forms its southernmost part, still bear the name of Punt.

"Amon, my father, should I send Egyptian soldiers to the East?"
The god, through the priest, answered "Yes."

Was it not so, that if the soldiers found new treasures, a share would be given as an offering to Amon, or rather his priests, as a token of gratitude?

The questions and answers continue... Of course no one was fooled by this pretense. Tradition, however, demanded that the gods be consulted in this way, but the statues inhabited by the divinities would, of course, only communicate with the priests.

"I am of the kings of justice"

Tutankhamen now had to pay homage to the god.

He was brought a bull, with its right horn tied by a rope to the right hind leg. The king placed a lasso around its horns, then the animal was turned over and its legs bound by the priests. The holy butcher stepped forward and slit the animal's throat from ear to ear. Dismembered in accordance with a time-honored ritual, the animal was offered as a meal to the god.

Before returning to the Palace, the king made his way to an esplanade behind the temple, which was the seat of the Court of Justice. It was customary for the Pharaoh to attend its sessions from time to time to enhance the solemnities of the proceedings by his presence. At a respectful distance a crowd of onlookers had gathered around the president of the court, the judges and scribes.

The men on trial on this occasion had been accused of having robbed tombs. It was such a commonplace offense that the Pharaoh was asked to hear only the crimes committed in the "true places"—the tombs of the great. The riches which they contained offered a great temptation. Almost every night mummies were stripped of their jewels, tombs were plundered. Often the thieves were in league with the priests or custodians of the tombs, whom they paid dearly for their complicity.

Making his way through the crowd of onlookers, who had prosternated themselves before him, Tutankhamen took his place beside the High Priest, who acted as Chief Justice. To the judges, the king addressed the traditional words, found in the *Abbot Papyrus*:

"Be compassionate; do not chastise the innocent; I am of the kings of Justice."

The court then resumed its proceedings, Tutankhamen attending until sentence had been passed. For many, this meant prison; for priests, hanging; for others, mutilation or beating, depending on the seriousness of the offense.

Afterwards, Tutankhamen hurried back to the Palace. For that same day he was to confer upon his loyal friend Huy the title of Viceroy of Kush, thereby appointing him Governor of Nubia.

"Take this hook which is the emblem of the Viceroy of Kush"

Huy belonged to one of the greatest noble families of Egypt, a man who had proved his worth and whose status was evident from the titles conferred upon him: "Fan-bearer at the King's right hand," and also, "Hero of His Majesty's cavalry." Moreover, he

knew Nubia well, since he had served under the Viceroy appointed
by Amenhotep III.

Tutankhamen had wished his investiture to be a most solemn
ceremony.

On the ground floor of the Palace, in the great chamber opposite
the banqueting hall, the Pharaoh took his seat on the throne,
beneath a canopy supported by stucco columns painted green, blue
and yellow. He wore a robe of pleated linen and the blue leather
crown *(kheperesh)* which symbolized the Pharaoh's command of his
earthly kingdom. In his right hand he carried the whip and the hook,
in his left the sign of life.

The officers opened the huge doors. Huy, who—as a mark of
special favor, wore his sandals, entered and bowed down before the
King. Also wearing a pleated robe, he carried, as a symbol of office,
the *flabellum*—a huge fan of peacock feathers and lotus leaves.

The voice of the master of ceremonies was heard:

"You now have the control over the region from Nekhen to
Napata." And Huy to reply: "May Amon grant all that you have
ordained, Oh, Sovereign and Master!"

Then he was handed the symbol of office.

"Take this hook, which is the emblem of the Viceroy of Kush,
from Nekhen to Napata."

The ceremony had come to an end. Huy bowed and took leave
of the King. He walked to the Temple of Amon, to give thanks. He
then went to the banks of the Nile, where a huge fleet awaited
him. While his magnificent vessel weighed anchor and set sail for
Nubia, dancers gave a graceful performance on the riverbank.

All the tributes of the South

As soon as he had set foot on Nubian soil, Huy, an intelligent and efficient man by nature, set to work with enthusiasm.

As he saw it, his first task was to collect taxes, for the coffers of the Pharaoh were empty. The Asian vassals had revolted against Ikhnaton in the latter years of his reign, had ceased to pay their tributes, or at best did so only occasionally.

Seconded by the Nubian princes educated at the Pharaoh's court, Huy restored peace and prosperity. He traveled the length and the breadth of the land to boost the confidence of workers and craftsmen alike.

He opened up new mines. He sent his men down south to hunt elephants, panthers and giraffes. On the Nile, boats carried huge trunks of ebony and mahogany. In the skilled hands of Nubian jewelers and craftsmen precious metals and rare woods were transformed into objects of exquisite beauty.

And soon Huy returned to Thebes bearing these tributes from the South.

To welcome him, Tutankhamen had his throne put up in the great courtyard of the Palace, because Huy had written that he would be bringing large quantities of treasures of all kinds.

Huy stepped forward, bearing the *flabellum* and the hook. He introduced to the King the nobles of Upper Nubia. The first to be introduced was the Prince of Kush, vassal of the Pharaoh. He wore a white pleated robe in the Egyptian style, and his arms were adorned with bracelets. A small crown perched askew on his wig made him look rather funny, this the more so as he visibly made an effort to adopt as noble and dignified a bearing as possible.

The Nubian nobles placed before Tutankhamen gold, large quantities of bloodstones, animal skins and the famous oxen of Kush, used for ceremonies or sacrifices.

The nobles were followed by the Prince of Miam, Hekanefer. Brought up in the *kep*, he had been a school companion of Tutankhamen. He bowed low before his friend, the King. Two other princes of Wawat, or Lower Nubia, accompanied him. All three wore the ceremonial dress of the chiefs of Wawat: a panther-skin cloak and a headdress of ostrich plumes.

They too laid out tributes at the sovereign's feet. First came rings and bags of gold dust, mountains of jasper, urns overflowing with cornelian and magnificent elephant tusks. Then they displayed the pieces of furniture they had brought him: chairs, beds, tables and folding chairs—all made of rare woods.

Lastly, with great ceremony, the Pharaoh was presented with a masterpiece of Nubian craftmanship: set on a long tray was a model of the local landscape, a model fashioned of precious metals and jewels. In the middle of a forest of date-palms, giraffes raised their heads to reach the fruit, while Nubians were attending to their occupations.

Huy had performed very well. As a token of his gratitude, Tutankhamen placed around his neck strands and strands of gold necklaces which covered his chest.

The Viceroy and his escort withdrew. Tutankhamen remained for a while in the courtyard and gazed in wonder at the treasures of Nubia which were spread out at his feet.

The lengthy ceremony had tired the young king. Leaving all these riches where they were, he went to rest. Tomorrow, another busy day lay ahead of him, a day devoted entirely to Amon.

Transforming ruins into "eternal monuments"

Alone in the penumbra of his room, Tutankhamen contemplated the task he had accomplished by restoring the worship of Amon whose unchallenged supremacy would be solemnly celebrated the following day.

He recalled that at the start of his reign, edged on by the priests and by Horemheb, he had decreed that he would make the "ruins flower anew" to become again the "eternal monuments."

These monuments and shrines had become a pitiful sight. Plundered, abandoned, decaying, they had been grown over by vegetation.

The young king gathered the scattered priests of Amon and also appointed others, generously bestowing on them goods of all kinds as is written on the great *stele* of Karnak. He repaired the effigies of Amon which had been desecrated on the orders of the "heretic" Ikhnaton.

Tutankhamen recalled his many journeys, especially at the start of his reign. Across the length and breadth of the country, he had visited the restored temples and paid homage to Amon.

The most beautiful holiday of Egypt

It was principally in Thebes, Luxor and Karnak that he had erected most of his constructions. At Luxor, Tutankhamen had organized the most beautiful holiday of Egypt. The feast of Amon was held each year in the month of *paophi*, the second month of the flood, and it lasted for eleven days. For now the statues of Amon in the shape of Tutankhamen abounded in these three places. But the young king had not forgotten Nubia. At Kawa, beyond the third waterfall, about 650 miles south of Thebes, he restored the temple which his father had built and erected another. And, in order to demonstrate his keen interest in Nubia, he had built a new temple at Faras, to the south of Abu-Simbel.

The many temples that had been built or rebuilt! Few Pharaohs have erected so many in so short a time.

Before his mind's eye the King relives all these inaugurations, always making the same ritual gestures. He would spread some incense, then, holding a long stick and a white club, he would raise his right arm in the direction of the temple and, by this gesture hand over the building "to its master."

"I hope that Amon is satisfied with me," muses the Pharaoh as he falls asleep.

The holy journey

The next day, Tutankhamen boards a huge boat, its silver hull decorated with gold. In its center stands the tabernacle made of electrum and housing the statue of Amon. On the bank of the Nile, the high priest is chanting a hymn to the glory of Tutankhamen who has pleased the gods. Priestesses wave their tambourines, dancers click their castanets. The people rejoice.

The ship which carries Tutankhamen and his son Nepkheprure-Tutankhamen glides down the river from Karnak to Luxor. For this is the "holy journey" during which the King shows his god all that he has done for him—scene later to be immortalized by artists on the walls of the temple of Luxor. Later on the vessel returns to Karnak and the statue of Amon is taken back to its *naos*.

Tonight, the weary Tutankhamen has the feeling that he has accomplished his task.

CHAPTER V

THE DEATH OF TUTANKHAMEN

> *"He will journey to Abydos, the Kingdom of*
> *Osiris. He will knock at the door of the*
> *Kindgom of Justice and, before the judges*
> *of Osiris, he will declare that his conscience*
> *is clear: 'I come as a true spirit, bringing*
> *justice to him who loves it.'"*

Extract from Chapter LXV of the
Book of the Dead

FOR some time already, Tutankhamen has found his duties to have become increasingly burdensome. He is getting more exhausted every day. Suddenly, his health begins to deteriorate. At Karnak, in front of the *naos* containing the statue of Amon, the priests endlessly repeat the incantations from the "mystical treatise." And as every hour is protected by a specific deity, the incantations change every hour.

Addressing the deity of the twelfth hour, the priest exclaims: "Protect him from all enemies and evil shadows!"

Emetics, enemas and magic formulas to cure Tutankhamen

While the temples echoed to the sound of endless prayers, the doctors were busy with the Pharaoh. Their knowledge was very limited: they had studied medical books supposedly of divine origin, as well as the remedies of the best doctors of the time, the Syrians and the Phoenicians.

In a society as advanced as that of Ancient Egypt, the doctors knew little about anatomy. This may seem paradoxical, since hundreds of corpses were cut up each day in the course of mummification. This humble task was peformed by embalmers and magicians, who were, as a result, shunned by the rest of society.

The doctors *(saumu)* who surround the king were many in number. In Ancient Egypt there were no general practitioners, only specialists. According to the *Ebers Papyrus* they prescribed remedies so that "the good, fragrant breath of the north wind would enter the right ear of Tutankhamen and go (...) to his heart (...) whose perpetual beating will carry the breath of life throughout his body." They administered emetics and enemas, which were so commonplace that there were over 170 formulas for them. The most usual of such rectal injections was warm goat's milk mixed with honey, or human milk with oil and salt added.

While the *saumu* administered the enema, the exorcist placed his hands on the king's stomach and uttered this formula, contained in the *Berlin Papyrus*: "Remove from this belly, oh hidden poison, the ills which afflicted Ment, son of Ment!"

In desperation,
they summon the sorcerer

The body of the boy king was wracked with pain.

The exorcist, called in once more, made him swallow a small ball of clay impregnated with herbs. While the unfortunate Pharaoh swallowed this bitter pill, the exorcist recited a new formula that went with its absorption. But the patient's sufferings grew worse and a specialist for pains was sent for. He crushed oxhorn and incense, mixed this with beer, and offered this revolting mixture to the king.

Despite all this medical attention, the king's condition worsened each day. On his chest, weak from coughing and fever, poultices followed after every sort of emollient. The helpless Tutankhamen swallowed the strangest potions, like the one mentioned in the *Ebers Papyrus*:

"Plant of Osiris (liana), heart of Bubastis (saffron), blood of Osiris and eye of Seth."

But as the patient was getting worse, the exorcist was called back. He adressed the spirits and told them that their evil powers could not harm the King, since he was protected by the gods. But the evil spirits are not to be convinced...

In any case, the doctors believed that all men—from the Pharaoh to the humblest of mortals—did not die, but were killed by some creature from the invisible world, be it demon, avenging angel or the spirit of the dead Pharaoh. They wonder whether Amon was not taking revenge on Tutankhamen for the sacrilege committed by Ikhnaton.

In desperation, they summon the sorcerer. He bent over the patient and uttered a few mysterious words:

"Oh, hostile spirit, do not take his heart! Do not attack his flesh! Do nothing to harm him!"

The dying Tutankhamen sees the mountains of Thebes on the horizon

Tutankhamen felt his life ebbing away, but he was not afraid of death. Like all Egyptians, he knew that at birth each person received a *Ka* which not only stayed beside him during his lifetime but also survived his death.

Since his childhood, the priests and all that he had read had taught him that dying was simply passing over to the *Ka*. This spirit grew up with the individual, but did not grow old. He must have recalled the fresco on which the wizened face of the aged King Hur seemed to be illuminated by his youthful *Ka*, which followed him. On the pyramids it had been written for thousands of years:

"All who pass over, journey to the other world with their *Ka*. You too must pass over with your *Ka!*"

Tutankhamen's only regret was to have to leave behind his young wife Ankhsenamon. She had born him no heir, and her situation would be far from enviable.

With a look of death on his face, the young Pharaoh turned towards the mountains of Thebes. There, on the horizon, his last resting-place was being prepared. There would be no more intrigues or disloyalty; he would no longer have to satisfy the demands of an ambitious and vindictive priesthood; there would be no more audiences, no more judgments, no more temples to be built. He remembered the words of the dying Ikhnaton: "Death brings peace, it is like the sailor coming home from the sea."

The infinite joys of the other world

For a brief moment, he saw the form of Ankhsenamon standing before him.

She was so young and Tutankhamen knew that, since his illness, intrigues had multiplied within the palace. The bent back of the aged Ay becomes straighter each day. Priests and courtiers alike already treated him as if he were the heir to the throne.

To forget his helplessness, Tutankhamen turned his thoughts to the other world which he would soon inhabit. This was every man's dream: to attain immortal life, not just for the spirit but for the body as well. He had often read the old texts describing the delights awaiting him, and which are depicted so vividly in the *Anastasi IV*

Papyrus: "The joy of Amon is in your heart, and you will spend your days in joy until you reach eternal bliss. Your mouth is firm, your limbs are agile and your eyes see clearly... You go on board your cedar-wood boat... and you arrive at your own perfect resting-place. Your mouth will be filled with wine, beer, bread, meat and cakes; oxen will be sacrificed and jars of wine will be opened; the sounds of sweet music will greet you... You are whole and your enemy is vanquished. No man can speak against you, for you are in the presence of the gods and your voice is just."

The death of Tutankhamen remains a mystery

Before reaching this eternal bliss, Tutankhamen would have to appear before his divine judges. They would weigh up the good and evil deeds during his life on earth.

The young king was not afraid. He knew that to attain eternal life, it was enough to know the prayers and rites, and the High Priest would give him the *Book of the Dead* to guide him along the right road.

Already he could see himself before his judges. He would only mention sins which he had not committed, as was written in the *Book of the Dead*. He would say: "I have done no wrong, I have committed no acts of violence, I have not stolen nor have I put anyone to death. I have caused no grief. I have loved god. I am pure, I am pure!"

Thot, the god of wisdom, would place the king's heart on one side of the scales, and an image of Truth on the other.

As he lay on his deathbed, the young king felt that the judgment would be in his favor. Then Thot and Anubis would lead him to a river, where he would go on board a boat which would take him to the fields of Ialu, the resting-place where life, it seemed, was so good.

His huge eyes closed. The face of the Pharaoh became even more handsome once all pain had ceased and the calm of eternal sleep had relaxed his features.

What was the cause of his death? Was it tuberculosis, as some have claimed, or that physical debility which seems to have been common among the later members of the XVIIIth dynasty? Was he assassinated? Or poisoned? Many theories have been put forward to explain the death of the boy king.

It was around January, 1343 B.C., when Tutankhamen finally set off on his journey to the fields of Ialu. The fruit and flowers placed in his tomb allow us to fix an approximate date. In Egypt, cornflowers and mandrakes reach the peak of their growth in March or April. We can place his actual death some 70 days earlier—the time taken by the process of mummification.

"You are now young forever"

Tutankhamen was laid out, naked, in an underground chamber. The process of transformation was about to begin. The king's body would become that of a god, resurrected for all eternity.

Around the body bathed in candlelight, the master of ceremonies, a priest, a surgeon and the assistants set to work.

By means of a curved iron instrument, the brain was removed through the nostrils. Then certain plants were placed inside the skull to dissolve what was left.

An incision about 4 inches long was made on the left side of the abdomen with a piece of obsidian from Ethiopia. While the priest recited prayers, the heart, lungs, liver and intestines were removed. The inside of the body was washed with palm wine, then filled with crushed myrrh and various aromatic plants.

No organ which would putrefy rapidly was left in place, and the others were given a treatment which would prevent them from decomposing.

The body of the king was shaved before being plunged into a vat of sodium to absorb the humidity.

Those present slowly backed out of the chamber. The body of their master would remain there for 70 days.

After this time, the king's body was washed and placed on a bed to dry. Then the assistants stuffed the chest, stomach and part of the face with perfumed sawdust and fine pieces of linen. They placed his legs together and crossed his arms on his chest in the traditional posture of dead Pharaohs. The goldsmiths would then enter to make a mould of the king's corpse.

"Whoever recites this chapter after having been purified will be reborn"

Since Tutankhamen had no son, it was the aged Ay who presided over the ritual of mummification.

The moment had come to wrap the body. Hundreds of yards of linen bandages were needed to cover it completely. Each finger and toe was wrapped separately, next the limbs, and finally the trunk itself.

While this was being done, the priest chanted the traditional prayer: "Whoever recites this chapter after having been purified in the sodium water will be reborn after burial."

The bandages were coated with ointments designed to restore life to the body. The face was covered by a mask, and the toes and fingers were encased in gold sheaths upon which the goldsmiths had engraved the shape of the nail and the first joint.

Why did the embalmers shave the king's head, as if he were a priest? Why did the garment which they put on him have two straps as if he were a god, instead of the one strap usually reserved for Pharaohs? Was Tutankhamen already considered to be a god? It is only a theory, but perhaps it explains why the robbers who broke into his tomb stole many things, but left the mummy intact.

The diadem was placed on the king's head. His neck was protected by several necklaces and about 20 amulets. These were made of gold and precious stones, and fastened around the king's neck with gold threads.

Between each layer of bandages the body was decorated with jewelry, necklaces, pectorals and golden gorgets. Against his left thigh was placed a gold dagger in a gold sheath, and against his right thigh, an iron dagger—at that time a rare and precious metal. These weapons were to kill any demons he might meet on his journey.

In accordance with tradition,
the queen keeps vigil over the body for 70 days

The Pharaoh's body was then wrapped in a large linen shroud, and his face was covered by a golden mask which was a lifelike image of his features. The eyes and eyebrows were of blue glass paste. The hair was encrusted with the same material. Around his neck were placed three necklaces, one of white gold, one of red gold and one of blue porcelain.

Sewn onto the fabric on his breast, two gold hands clutched the emblems of royalty. Beneath these, a gold breast-plate depicted a bird, *Ba*, with its wings outstretched. Then the shroud was fastened with strands of gold ribbon bearing sacred inscriptions, such as: "Oh, Osiris, Tutankhamen, you are traveling towards Re!"

Tutankhamen was then brought back to the Palace, where he lay in state.

For the past 70 days, as was the custom, the young queen had not left the chamber.

Despite her great grief, she had to face facts. Since there was no heir to the throne, she has only three months in which to marry a prince in order to stay in power.

Horemheb foils the queen's plan

The annals of Murshil II, son of Suppiluliuma, King of the Hittites, miraculously discovered in the ruins of the ancient Hittite capital, relate the strange behavior of the queen after her husband's death:

"The Queen of Egypt, now a widow, sent an ambassador to my father and addressed him in these terms: 'My husband is dead and I have no son. If you send me one of your sons, I will make him my husband, since I have no wish to marry one of my own subjects...'"

This was an unprecedented request. The Hittite King was so taken aback that he sent his own ambassador to Egypt to make certain that the message was correct.

Ankhsenamon wrote a second letter confirming that the request was genuine and repeated it:

"Why do you say: 'They are trying to deceive me'? If I had a son, would I have suffered the humiliation of writing to a foreign ruler? Give me one of your sons as my husband and he will be King of Egypt." To offer the throne to a foreigner was such a bold stroke that it cannot have been the queen's own idea. The scheme must have had the backing of the aged Ay, who probably sought an alliance with a powerful nation in an attempt to block the accession of Horemheb. It was no doubt with the latter in mind that the queen had written that she did not wish to marry one of her own subjects.

The Hittite King did send one of his sons to Egypt. But General Horemheb, intensely patriotic was determined to prevent at all costs the rule of a foreign prince. He charged several trusted men with the mission of killing the young prince. He was murdered before he reached Thebes.

The queen's hopes were crushed. She would have to rule with a co-regent. On the eve of her husband's funeral, she chose Ay as co-regent. Did she marry him? So some have claimed, but there is nothing to support this theory, and one significant fact which seems to disprove it: Ay was to make his wife, Ti, a queen; her name was found in an inscription in Ay's tomb.

Dressed in mourning, a white band around her forehead, the queen sobs...

On a warm morning in April, 1343 B.C., the doors of the Palace swung open. The Pharaoh's mummy had been placed on a bier in the shape of a boat. Placed on a sled drawn by bulls, the royal body slowly left the Palace grounds.

Behind it followed an impressive procession, at its head the highest officials and priests, then the courtiers carrying everything that the king would need in the other world: food, the kings customary furniture and the funerary furnishings proper.

The drivers urged on the bulls: "To the West, you bulls who draw the bier, to the West! Your master is behind you."

The young queen advanced, leading the group of women. Wearing mourning robes, a white band around her forehead, like the other members of the funeral procession, she was sobbing gently.

While the official mourners wailed and rent their clothes, a few intimates of Tutankhamen, whose grief was, no doubt, sincere, chanted the traditional words with which the living address the departed: "To the West! To the West!"

The crowd looks up to the sky, trying to see Ba, the bird symbolizing the soul

The procession reached the Nile. People and treasures were loaded onto barges and boats.

At the head of this flotilla, a blue barge carried the wailing mourners, towing behind it a smaller vessel adorned with a huge silver lotus blossom at each end. In the center of this boat, beneath a canopy, lay the king's mummy.

On the boats, the priests intoned the words of the funeral service.

Kneeling beside her husband's remains, Ankhsenamon sobbed: "Oh, my beloved husband, stay here. Alas, you are crossing the river. Oh sailors, do not hasten! He is leaving for the land of eternity."

The procession had by now reached the burial ground. The royal vessel was hoisted onto a sled which would be drawn by the leaders of the nation.

They reached at last the Valley of the Kings, the burial ground of almost all the members of the XVIIIth Dynasty.

In front of the tomb, the king's mummy is placed upright. The High Priest and Ay—acting for the first time as ruler—purified the mummy, then placed on it the "crown of justification," made of lotus blossoms and olive leaves. Now Ay, wielding the adze *(kheperesh)*, feigned to be opening the king's mouth. Instinctively, the crowd looked up to the leaden sky, hoping to see Ba, the bird which symbolized the soul. The king's soul, free at last, would live its spiritual life among the gods, while his body would remain in the cool of the tomb.

CHAPTER VI

THE VENGEANCE OF HOREMHEB

*"The officials of the royal household walked in
procession with Tutankhamen, King Osiris,
towards the West."*

Inscription on a wall of
Tutankhamen's burial chamber

THE ritual opening of the mouth took place in the open air,
for no chapel had been built at the entrance to the tomb.
What was the reason for this departure from tradition,
and the relatively modest proportions of the tomb itself?

Tutankhamen had died at an age when death was unexpected—except, perhaps, in the case of a Pharaoh...

70 days to prepare the tomb of Tutankhamen

Supposing that Tutankhamen had a tomb built for himself, was it the long tube-shaped grave in which Horemheb was later buried, or perhaps that of Ay?

But when the Pharaoh died, neither of these hypogea was ready. The rapid progression of his illness had clearly taken the royal entourage by surprise. Normally, between the death of a king and his burial, a long period was allowed for the lavish decoration and furnishing of his last resting-place. But the Palace was clearly anxious to proceed with the funeral. Were they afraid that Horemheb might seize power? Or was it simply Ay who could not wait to wear the double crown?

Whatever the reason, the artists and craftsmen only had the time needed for embalming—70 days—to prepare the tomb. They chose a relatively small tomb, but one which was almost complete and designed for a king. It was probably the tomb which Ay had intended for himself, since certain members of the royal family had the privilege of building vaults of this design.

Under the protection of four goddesses

While the ceremony of purification was being performed, the Pharaoh's possessions were being transported on an endless chain of carts.

In a small room leading to the burial chamber were placed the objects necessary for the reconstitution of the body. The most impressive of these was the wooden tabernacle decorated with gold, containing four vessels with their lids in the shape of a face. With its carved cornice of serpents crowned by the disk of the sun, this box was covered in hieroglyphics and religious scenes. The four goddesses, Isis, Nephthys, Neith and Selkit, in high relief, protect the tabernacle with their outstretched arms. Inside, a coffer of alabaster contained four vessels of the same material. On the side of each vessel was an image of each goddess: Isis to protect the liver, Nephthys the lungs, Neith for the stomach and Selkit for the intestines. The king's heart had been put back in his body.

The priests began a ceremony which would allow these organs and the body to be joined together once more. This is why there was no door between this room and the burial chamber itself.

Beside the southern wall were placed seven boxes, each one a *naos* containing the statue of a spirit or god made of gilded or ebonized wood. Their eyes were of obsidian, alabaster or glass paste.

Chariots, bows and arrows to protect the king in his tomb

Then a whole miniature fleet was placed in the tomb. Composed of different types of vessel painted in vivid colors, this fleet would allow the dead monarch——a foetus once more——to complete his journey within the womb of the mother goddess. To underline this symbolism, two mummified foetuses were also placed in the chamber.

At the southwestern corner, a box bearing the form of Osiris was filled with earth soaked in Nile water. Seeds of corn were sowed in this earth. They would germinate, and the young corn would symbolise the rebirth of Osiris and, at the same time, the resurrection of the dead king.

No doubt to assist this process two small sarcophagi were also placed here——one containing a gold statuette of Amenhotep III and the other a lock of Teje's hair.

In the northeastern corner of the room were heaped caskets containing the *ushabti*——mummy-like effigies of the king.

Since the darkness of the tomb would be crowded with evil spirits, chariots, bows and arrows, which the god Ched would use to protect the king from any dangers before his rebirth, were placed against the walls.

Many richly decorated coffers full of priceless jewelry were carried in next: a profusion of gold, glass-paste, lapis-lazuli, amethyst, cornelian and turquoise. The shapes of these jewels all represented the rebirth of the departed: eyes, scarabs, boats bearing a rising sun, etc.

It was in this chamber——or so the Egyptians believed——that the first stages of the transformation would take place. For this reason, a huge coffer of gilded wood was placed at the entrance; upon it lay a black wooden statue of the dog Anubis, his head turned towards the burial chamber. This dog, to whom the royal child had often been compared at his birth, represented the imminent journey from darkness to the light of eternal life.

"Oh king, come in peace!
Oh god and protector of the country"

The paintings were scarcely dry on the walls of the golden chamber destined to receive the king's body. They stood out vividly against a heavy ochre background. On the left side of the north wall, Tutankhamen was portrayed standing before the "ladies of heaven"; the goddess Nut stepped forward to greet him. In another picture, the Pharaoh, with his *Ka* beside him, embraced the god Osiris as if he wanted to merge into him. To the right, Ay, dressed as a king, performed the ritual opening of the mouth.

At the far end, a fresco depicted the funeral procession itself. The words of the mourners were written beside their mouths: "Oh king, come in peace! Oh god and protector of the country!"

The west wall was divided into horizonal strips or small pictures representing the first hour of the "funeral night," which the Pharaoh was about to enter.

A marvelous coffin of solid gold

Ankhsenamon went into the tomb, accompanied by two of her sisters. They were followed by Ay, the priests and two of Tutankhamen's best friends—General Nakim, and Maya the treasury official, who had supervised the preparation of the tomb.

The mummy was placed in a marvelous coffin of solid gold. Before the lid was closed, the king's body was once more coated with ointments. It was then covered with a large red shroud and a necklace of flowers and leaves was placed around the neck. The first coffin was placed inside the second, made of gilded wood and decorated with red jasper and turquoises. Upon this second coffin was placed a garland of willow and olive leaves, as well as petals of cornflower and lotus. A third plain gold coffin received the other two. Around the sacred cobra and vulture which were part of the headdress, a final "crown of justification" was placed.

This triple coffin, swathed in several layers of linen, was placed in a sarcophagus of pink sandstone. Slaves used pulleys to lower the lid. Through clumsiness, or perhaps lack of space (there were less than 30 inches between the sarcophagus and the wall), the lid was lowered too quickly and was cracked. The crack was hastily plastered over by the slaves and painted over to hide the damage.

Isis and Nephthys spread their wings as if to give the breath of life to the dead king

Once the sandstone sarcophagus had been sealed, it was hidden beneath four shrines of gilded wood, each with a design representing a different aspect of the king.

The first represented the old palace of the rulers of the North, "Per-Nu" (the house of flame), where Tutankhamen had received his crowns. At the corners were figures of Isis and Nephthys with their wings outstretched as if to give the breath of life to the dead king. Inside, just one chapter——the most important——of the *Book of the Dead* was inscribed. When archeologists opened the tomb many centuries later, they were surprised not to find the whole book written on papyrus, as was customary.

The priests assembled the four panels of the shrine by fixing wooden pegs into metal hooks and then putting the roof in place. Hurriedly, they assembled the second and third shrines, the latter resembling the Southern Temple, "Per-Ur," and the former decorated with pictures of funeral rites and evil spirits like those described in the *Book of the Dead*. Beneath the roof, the king was depicted among the divine birds as a falcon, his wings outstretched.

The third shrine also bore pictures of Tutankhamen accompanied by Isis, and walking towards Osiris to take his place on the boat of the gods.

The feasts of Sed

Once this third shrine had been completed, various objects were placed beside its walls. There were sticks with handles bearing effigies of the Pharaoh, ceremonial batons of red wood incrusted with ivory, and various weapons. Pots containing ointments were also left there, one depicting the "union of the Two Lands"—in other words Upper and Lower Egypt. Another, cylindrical in shape, was surmounted by a lion couchant baring its tongue.

The fourth and last shrine depicted the pavilion of jubilee celebrations, or feasts of *Sed*, during which the Pharaoh renewed his powers after simulating death.

The golden chamber is plunged forever into darkness

Next the attendants placed beside the outer walls ten paddles to assist the Pharaoh in his voyage across the oceans of the other world. The sacred goose covered by a veil, was placed against the east wall.

Lastly, at the foot of the shrine, Ay placed wine jars and a bunch of pansies and olives handed to him by Ankhsenamon.

A final prayer was said while the last torch was extinguished. The golden chamber was plunged forever into darkness.

Hurriedly the masons constructed a simple wall of bricks to seal off the inner room from the antechamber. Once the entrance had been blocked up, the royal seals were affixed. Ay then had two magnificent statues of the Pharaoh placed in front of the wall. They were of black varnished wood, with gold sandals, pleated loincloth, ornate headdress and bracelets. The monarch held in his hands a gold lance and a gold club. These almost identical statues were most impressive, firstly because of their size (they were life-size), and secondly because the sculptor had given them incredibly realistic features. They bore the name of "The Royal Ka of Harakty, the Osiris Tutankhamen."

"May you live for millions of years, oh lover of Thebes!

It was now the antechamber, where these two statues stood, which became the scene of great activity. The servants were

weighed down by the multitude of objects which they carried. Ay
had ordered that all the furniture belonging to the Pharaoh should
be placed in his tomb. This was an unusual gesture, for in general
royal tombs contained only objects made specially for the funeral.

What was the reason for this departure from tradition? Did the
craftsmen not have enough time to make furniture worthy of a
king? Or did Ay wish to remove from sight any reminder of Tutankhamen?

The long line of servants brought in beds, stools and innumer-
able coffers made of wood or reeds. Then came flyswatters, vases,
sceptres, jewel caskets, and sticks with their handles in the shape
of African or Asian heads, to represent the peoples against whom
the Pharaoh had to defend his realm. Each of these objects was of
incredible beauty and opulence. Everything was there: precious
wood, gold, turquoise, ivory, enamel, lapis-lazuli.

Along the walls were golden chariots which had been dismantled. On their sides were engraved stylized floral motifs or historical scenes.

In the center, Ay placed the Pharaoh's throne, with a scene from
the royal couple's private life depicted on the back panel. Enamel,
turquoise and lapis-lazuli stood out against a brilliant gold background. The official throne, used by Tutankhamen for ceremonials,
was placed beside it.

At the entrance to the antechamber, a wonderful alabaster cup,
representing a lotus blossom, bore the inscription: "May your *Ka*
survive! May you spend millions of years, oh lover of Thebes,
seated, your face turned towards the north wind and your eyes
beholding happiness!"

In this room, Tutankhamen would be able to exercise his royal authority for all eternity.

The queen, with a graceful gesture, offers bunches of lotus blossoms to the king...

The servants were now ready to fill the last chamber of the tomb.

They installed an ebony throne inlaid with ivory, porcelain and precious stones. On the back panel, Tutankhamen and Ankhsenamon were portrayed in a familiar pose.

A gold-covered *naos* was decorated with numerous scenes in which the royal couple were always together. For the wife was considered to be the "favorite concubine" of the departed king. In one, the queen is shown offering flowers and perfumes to the king as a prelude to the act of love. In another, Tutankhamen was shooting duck with his bow, since they symbolized evil spirits who might threaten the royal marriage. This destruction of evil, in the form of wild birds, would explain the presence in this chamber of 278 arrows, numerous boomerangs, swords and shields.

On a large coffer with an ivory lid were the husband and wife, sitting under a canopy in a garden. The queen was offering the Pharaoh bunches of lotus blossoms and papyrus.

Tutankhamen had abandoned the heresy of his predecessor Ikhnaton to restore the cult of Amon. Here is shown the latter protecting the young Pharaoh. *The Louvre, Bulloz.*

All is set for the king's rebirth

These images of the queen in the tomb represented the possibility of the deceased being able to father a child, and thus be reborn.

Four beds were installed, two of ebony and two of wood. The king would be able to choose his nuptial couch.

As for the child of this union, he would be given the objects which the king himself had used during his childhood: his sling, his "lighter," his toy boxes, his linen chests.

Several sets of the *senet* game were laid out. Then 134 alabaster vases and receptacles containing oils and ointments were brought in. Last came the food: more than 100 baskets of grapes, melon seeds, mandrakes, not to mention three dozen jars of wine.

All was set for the king's rebirth.

Ay, master of Egypt

Ay casts a final glance at the room, then goes outside, escorted by the servants. The masons built another wall to seal off the chamber.

In front of the tomb, the slaves had already begun to serve the banquet. Where the royal mummy once rested, there now stood a statue of Tutankhamen to overlook the proceedings. A portion of each dish was offered first to the effigy.

The pitiful wailings of the mourners had long since died away. The air was now filled with joyful song: "Make the day happy, life is too short!"

Then the songs die away. Ay, who was the last to leave the tomb, makes his appearance. The guests greet him respectfully, for he is now the master of Egypt.

Maya protects the tomb of Tutankhamen

During his brief, inglorious reign—just four years—the tomb of Tutankhamen was robbed. The ointments and a large quantity of the priceless jewels were taken. Maya, the Treasury Secretary and loyal friend of Tutankhamen, sent inspectors into the tomb. They went in along a small tunnel dug by the robbers. They managed to put some things back in place, but had to return to the surface quickly because the air was so rare inside the tomb that they could not stay long enough to replace everything. To protect the tomb, Maya had the entrance covered with a huge layer of rocks. There was now no outward sign of a tomb.

What became of Ankhsenamon? She seems to have left the stage just as Tutankhamen passed into eternity, for nothing more is known about her.

The vengeance of Horemheb

After the death of Ay, Horemheb was to realize his lifelong ambition.

On a sunny day during the great feast of Opet, the priest wearing the mask of Horus presented him to Amon in the temple of Luxor, to consecrate him as king.

The cunning general became a Pharaoh by the grace of Amon, or, more precisely, of his priests.

He was a popular ruler. He restored the fortunes of the kingdom and became its first legislator. He had an edict engraved on the granite of Karnak decreeing a reform of the administration and the army, to restore them "to perfect order and integrity."

Horemheb was above all concerned to blot out forever anything which might recall the heresy of Ikhnaton and his followers. Tutankhamen had indeed restored the cult of Amon and built many temples, but the priests were not entirely satisfied. The god had regained prestige and power, but his revenge was still to come. Horemheb was to give this satisfaction to the priests who had made him Pharaoh.

On Horemheb's orders, the City of the Sun was destroyed, and the tomb of Ay plundered. Then the new Pharaoh turned his attention towards Tutankhamen. His seals were removed and replaced by those of the old general. The statues of the boy king were destroyed or disfigured—or even thrown into the Nile. This merciless process was carried to the farthest provinces. The tombs of the nobles who had served Tutankhamen were also plundered. All traces of the king's name were ruthlessly erased.

Struck from the list of Pharaohs

Why, amid this systematic persecution, did Horemheb respect the tomb of Tutankhamen? Was it perhaps because he gave him credit for the restoration of the cult of Amon? We do not know for sure. In any case, the boy king hardly was a threat. Horemheb had struck out all the records, chiseled into the walls of Karnak after the death of Amenhotep III. In the line of Pharaohs, Ikhnaton, Tutankhamen and Ay had disappeared and Horemheb was presented as the immediate successor of Amenhotep III.

Struck from the list of Pharaohs, Tutankhamen was also removed from the shrines. Without a name, he would be unable to receive any prayers or become the object of any cult.

It would be more than three thousand years before his tomb was discovered by archeologists who would—according to the teachings of Ancient Egypt, bring him back to life, simply by pronouncing his name.

PART TWO

THE MOST FABULOUS
ARCHEOLOGICAL DISCOVERY
OF ALL TIME

"I think that we were reluctant to break the seals,
for, from the moment we began to open the shrine,
we felt like intruders... In our imagination,
we could see opening up the doors of the other shrines,
one within another, until the last would reveal
the body of Tutankhamen."

Howard Carter

Chapter I

HOWARD CARTER,
THE DETERMINED ARCHEOLOGIST

"**E**GYPTOLOGY," wrote the English General Tomkyns Hilgrove Turner, "is not a science, it is a passion which overwhelms those who embrace it, to such an extent that they give up everything to devote themselves to it."

This was the case with the American lawyer Theodore Davis. In 1902 he left America, and for the next twelve years undertook vast excavations in the Valley of the Kings, the immense royal necropolis which lies along the left bank of the Nile opposite Thebes.

His efforts were often successful. In those twelve years, he discovered the tombs of Thutmose IV, Horemheb, Spitah, Queen Hatshepsut and, lastly, the joint tomb of Juja and Tuju, which was unusual in that it had not been plundered and contained mummies in an almost perfect state of preservation.

To help him with his research, Davis hired a young English archeologist, Howard Carter.

Carter, who had already worked with Flinders Petrie, had been in Egypt since 1890. At the time administrator of the Department of Antiquities, he assisted Davis for seven years.

An apparently insignificant discovery

In 1908 Davis and Carter made a discovery to which they attached little importance.

During one excavation, they found a cache of resin jars containing bundles of linen and other small objects.

By chance, these objects were sent to Sir Herbert Winlock, of the Metropolitan Museum in New York.

Some time later, the two archeologists received the news that the seal of Tutankhamen had been discovered on a blue earthenware goblet.

Davis, who felt that the Valley of the Kings had been exhausted of its treasures, chose to ignore this piece of news.

Carter, on the other hand, cherished a secret hope that one day he might discover the tomb of the king.

How could he find the tomb of Tutankhamen?

The following year, another find confirmed Carter's intuition.

In an underground chamber to the north of Horemheb's tomb, the searchers found a wooden casket containing pieces of gold foil and decorated with paintings in which the forms of Tutankhamen and his wife Ankhsenamon could clearly be seen.

A few weeks later, Carter found some pieces of pottery bearing the seal of Tutankhamen, as well as a linen head-shawl bearing the date: the 6th year of Tutankhamen.

Despite these finds, Davis was still convinced that the Valley of the Kings had nothing more to offer. He was not alone in this. Gaston Maspero, the Curator of the Cairo Museum, was less categorical in his opinion, but affirmed his belief that the tomb of Tutankhamen had probably been plundered by Horemheb, the real successor of the boy king, after the brief and troubled reign of the aged Ay.

Carter, however, was not discouraged. He was convinced that the tomb was somewhere in the Valley of the Kings, intact and inviolate. But how could he find it?

The first meeting of Carter and Carnarvon

Chance, as so often happens in archeology, was to make Carter's dream a reality.

Just before the outbreak of World War I, Maspero invited the young English archeologist to his house.

"I have just been visited by a Lord," explained Maspero, "Lord Carnarvon by name. He has come to Egypt to convalesce after a serious automobile accident. This wealthy man wants to undertake his own excavations, but his knowledge of archeology is strictly limited. He needs the assistance of a specialist like you. Would you agree to help him?"

Carter accepted without hesitation. A few days later he made the acquaintance of Lord Carnarvon.

Lord Carnarvon,
sportsman and art connoisseur

From the very beginning, Carter was charmed by the personality of the aristocrat.

"Ever since I was a young man," he said, "I have been interested in the arts. I am a great collector of ancient drawings and prints."

"Have you studied archeology?" asked Carter.

"No, not at all," answered Carnarvon. "After being educated by a private tutor, I was sent to Eton, following family tradition, and then to Trinity College, Cambridge. When my father died, I was 23. Thanks to the inheritance he left me, I led a rather wild life. I went racing, shooting and even took part in a round-the-world sailing race. And then, one day, I discovered cars. My driving license was the third one issued in Great Britain. One day, while I was driving home, my car skidded and I was seriously injured. My doctors advised me to convalesce in the south, and so I chose Egypt. I have been here since 1903, and, by accompanying one or two archeological missions, I discovered an activity which would satisfy my love of sport and my desire to take a serious interest in the arts."

Relations between the two men were excellent. During the first few months, Carnarvon became the keen pupil of Carter, whose explorations he financed to a certain extent.

Carter and Carnarvon
take over from Davis

When World War I broke out, Davis went back to America and gave up his concession to dig in the Valley of the Kings. Carter and Carnarvon decided to take it over.

Maspero, as controller of Egyptian antiquities, approved the concession, but could not help reminding the two explorers that the undertaking was extremely risky.

"You are chasing a mirage," he told them. "The tomb of Tutankhamen has almost certainly been plundered and destroyed."

"We shall see," replied Carter obstinately.

For technical reasons, work did not start in earnest until the autumn of 1917. And since there had been no topographical survey of the Valley of the Kings, Carter followed a hunch and chose a site for the dig. This area, within a triangle marked by the tombs of Rameses II, Meren-Ptah and Rameses VI, was carefully cleared.

Years of digging with no result

Hundreds of *fellahs* took part in the dig, clearing masses of sand and rocks.

During the year 1919, at the foot of the open tomb of Rameses VI, the searchers unearthed several workmen's huts built upon slabs of flint.

"I am sure that the tomb of Tutankhamen is near these huts,"

Carter confided to Lord Carnarvon. "They must have been used by the workmen who camouflaged the royal tomb."

Then, during the winter, a handful of funerary objects were discovered in a cache in the entrance to the tomb of Rameses VI. However, so as not to prevent tourists from visiting the tomb, the two archeologists postponed for the time being their investigation of this site.

Work did continue for two years in a small adjacent valley, near the tomb of Thutmose III, but without real success. The years went by, and in 1922 no find of any significance had been made and money was gradually running out.

One spot still remained unexplored: the site of the workmen's huts at the foot of the tomb of Rameses VI.

The two men conferred. Was it reasonable to devote more time and the little money that was left to this area. Would it not be better to explore a new one?

The last chance

Carter and Carnarvon—after much hesitation—decided to devote one more winter to their enterprise.

On November 1, 1922, Carter and a team of workmen started to dig. They made a trench from the northeastern corner of the tomb running south, and crossing at right angles the slate foundations of the huts.

Two days later, after having uncovered enough of these huts, Carter began the process of clearing and sifting.

When he arrived at the site the next morning, an unusual silence greeted him. All the workmen had stopped digging and were huddled in a group.

A flight of stairs

"What is happening?" asked Carter. "Why have you stopped work?"

"We have found a trench cut into the rock," answered Ahmed Gurgar, the foreman.

"Underneath the first hut," added one of the workers.

Carter could scarcely believe it. Had they found the precious tomb?

When he approached the site of this find, he could see a passage hollowed out of the rock a few yards from the entrance to the tomb of Rameses VI.

On the evening of November 5, all the rubble blocking the passage was cleared away, revealing the start of a flight of steps.

These steps led, without any possible doubt, to a tomb of some sort. Would it be the tomb of Tutankhamen? Was it still intact, or had it already been plundered?

Chapter II

TOMB OR CACHE?

THE opening unearthed by Carter went into the rock and led to a corridor ten feet high and six feet wide.

While the workmen were clearing the twelfth step, which led westward, they discovered a sealed door. Anxious to identify the seals, Carter approached the door and scratched away the earth still covering it with the palm of his hand. A jackal and nine captives were revealed. These were the seals of the most famous royal tombs.

Eager to know what lay beyond the door, Carter made a peephole beneath the heavy wooden lintel and discovered a corridor full of rocks.

Carter to Carnarvon:
"Have made wonderful discovery"

Resisting his impulse to carry on digging, Carter had the flight of stairs covered with earth.

"Anything," he wrote, "literally anything might lie beyond that passage, and it needed all my self-control to keep from breaking down the door and investigating then and there."

Carter decided to await the return of Lord Carnarvon, who was at that time in England. The next day, he sent him a telegram:

"At last have made wonderful discovery in valley; a magnificent tomb with seals intact; re-covered same for your arrival; congratulations."

On November 7, the news of the find went round the world and was splashed over the front page of all the papers. Congratulations, requests for information, and offers of assistance piled up on Carter's desk. He was taken aback by such publicity.

In order to strengthen the team of archeologists, Carter contacted Callender, a young man with whom he had already worked, asking him to come out.

On November 8, Callender arrived, and he and Carter awaited with impatience the return of Lord Carnarvon, who had sent them two telegrams that day: "Arriving soon" and "Will be in Alexandria 20th."

A wooden, multicolored statuette, inlaid with bronze and gold. It depicts the *ushabti* of Tutankhamen. The *ushabti*, of which there were 365, represented servants who, in lieu of the King, had to do every day throughout the year certain agricultural labors required of the Pharaoh in the land of the dead. *Ferni.*

The seals are broken

Burning with curiosity, Carter and Callender were obliged to wait for more than two weeks.

At last, on November 23, Lord Carnarvon, accompanied by his daughter, Lady Evelyn Herbert, arrived in the Valley of the Kings.

In the afternoon of the following day, the workmen uncovered the flight of steps once more. When the sixteenth step was cleared, the door appeared. This time, Carter, thanks to the broad daylight, was able to decipher the name of Tutankhamen near the bottom of the door.

His intuition had proven correct.

Excited by this discovery, the archeologists proceeded to examine the door. But their second discovery tempered their enthusiasm. A part of the door had clearly been removed and replaced several times.

So the tomb had been violated. The question was, to what extent? To find out they would have to go inside.

The next day the seals were broken. Before this, they had been copied and photographed. To protect the entrance Callender had made a wooden grille to replace the broken door.

The moment of truth

The nerves of the archeologists, already shattered by their previous discovery, received another rude shock: in the debris which covered the 24-foot corridor, they found several objects bearing the name of Tutankhamen, but also others bearing the names of Ikhnaton and Sakerez, and two scarabs with the names of Thutmose III and Amenhotep III.

Was it then just a cache, or the tomb of Tutankhamen?

On the following day, November 26, in the middle of the afternoon, behind more rubble appeared a second door sealed with the name of Tutankhamen. But here again, traces of robbers were evident.

Slowly, carefully, the last stones in front of this second door were cleared away.

This time, the moment of truth had arrived.

"It's wonderful!" exclaimed Carter

To find out what lay behind the door, Carter made a small hole in the top left-hand corner and poked through a small iron bar. There was no resistance.

He then slipped several candles through the hole to detect any foul gases. There was no reaction.

Carter enlarged the hole, and, with the aid of a torch, looked into the cavity.

Lord Carnarvon, his daughter as well as Callender and the others, crowded round him. "At first I could see nothing," wrote Carter. "The hot air escaping from the chamber caused the candle flame to flicker, but presently, as my eyes grew accustomed to the light, details of the room within emerged slowly from the mist, strange animals, statues, and gold—everywhere the glint of gold. For a

moment——an eternity it must have seemed to the others standing
by——I was struck dumb with amazement, and when Lord Carnarvon,
unable to stand the suspense any longer, inquired anxiously, 'Can
you see anything?' all I could do was to get out the words, 'Yes,
wonderful things.' Then, widening the hole a little further, so that
we could both see, we inserted an electric torch.''

"The effect was overwhelming"

The room, lit for the first time in more than three thousand
years, measured about 30 feet by 10 feet.

The archeologists were literally petrified by the sight which met
their eyes. Opposite them, placed against the wall, were three huge
gilt couches. To the right, two life-size black statues stood facing
each other like sentinels, the protective sacred cobra on their foreheads.

On the floor was an amazing profusion of chests, alabaster
vases, bunches of dried flowers, furniture, chariots and portraits of
the king.

"Let the reader imagine how the objects appeared to us as we
looked down upon them from our spy-hole in the blocked doorway,
casting the beam of light from our torch (. . .) from one group of
objects to another, in a vain attempt to interpret the treasure that
lay before us. The effect was bewildering, overwhelming. I suppose
we had never formulated exactly in our minds just what we had
expected or hoped to see, but certainly we had never dreamed of
anything like this: a roomful——a whole museumful, it seemed, of

objects——some familiar, but some the like of which we had never seen, piled one upon another in seemingly endless profusion."

One thing perplexed them: there was no sarcophagus or mummy.

Suddenly, the beam of light picked out a third sealed door, between the two statues. What lay behind it?

Suddenly one of the archeologists gave a shout

The next morning, after having spent the night asking question after question about the nature of their find (was it a cache or a tomb?), the team of archeologists set to work once more.

Callender improved the lighting by running cables from the main electrical system of the Valley, while Carter and Carnarvon made copies of the seal impressions on the second door before unfastening it.

Around noon, the second door was unblocked. One by one they carefully entered the chamber. Near the entrance, a vessel containing the mortar used to seal the door partly covered a garland of flowers left as a token of farewell to the Pharaoh. On the walls, fingerprints were visible on the paintings.

Suddenly, one of the archeologists, who had bent down to look under the three gilt couches at the far end of the antechamber, let out a shout: "A hole... there's a hole!"

One of the assistants immediately brought a light and directed it through the opening. A second room, smaller than the antechamber, emerged from the darkness.

Its contents were more varied than those of the first room. Every-thing was in disorder, and many objects were broken. Had the rob-bers been surprised and forced to flee without taking anything?

A more careful examination of the third sealed door seemed to confirm this theory. Another sealed opening (probably sealed by the custodian of the City of the Dead, who had discovered the thieves at work) was clearly visible at floor level. There was no possible doubt—the robbers had been here too.

CHAPTER III

A GOLDEN WALL

ALTHOUGH they were eager to remove the third door to discover the extent of the robbery, Carter and Carnarvon decided to proceed slowly. They would systematically clear the antechamber and the small annex.

The contents of these two rooms were to provide information of incalculable value about Egyptian civilisation.

International co-operation on a grand scale

This operation was carried out by the two archeologists with painstaking efficiency.

Carter and Carnarvon set up a photographic studio in the chambers of Queen Teje, and a laboratory in the tomb of Set II, which were close at hand.

International co-operation on a grand scale was organized.

Eminent experts were called in, such as Harry Burton of New York, the photographer; the two artists Hall and Hauser; Arthur A. Mace of the Metropolitan Museum; Professor Breasted of the University of Chicago, an expert on seals; Professor Alan Gardiner, a specialist in hieroglyphics; and Alfred Lucas, director of the Department of Chemistry in the National Museum of Cairo.

For over ten weeks, the treasures contained in the two rooms were gradually removed with scientific precision.

Certain objects were preserved *in situ*, while others were covered in paraffin wax and fixed to a solid base to prevent any deterioration in transit.

By mid-February, 1923, the anteroom and the annex had been completely cleared.

Archeologists and officials
wait in the antechamber

At last the wall separating the antechamber from the burial chamber could be demolished.

On February 17, 1923, at two in the afternoon, about twenty people were invited to witness this event. There were Lord Carnarvon and his daughter, of course, as well as Callender and the other experts who had combined their efforts to clear the two rooms.

Also present were the Egyptian Minister of Public Works, Abd el Halim Pacha Suliman; the Director General of the Administration of Antiquities, Lacau; two Englishmen, William Garstin and Charles Rust; Lythgoe, the Curator of Egyptian Antiquities of the Metropolitan Museum; Winlock; Mervin Herber; Richard Bethell; Engelbach, the Inspector General of the Administration of Antiquities, and lastly the representative of the official Egyptian Press.

Chairs had been placed in the antechamber, and Callender had installed electricity so that officials and experts alike would wait in the best possible conditions.

Their conversation was animated, and they each speculated about the possible contents of the room they supposed to be the burial chamber.

A wall of gold

It was at this moment, that Carter, amid an impressive silence, approached the door. The harsh light of the electric lamps revealed the partition which he was about to remove.

Slowly, with great difficulty, he removed the stones one at a time. It was important, throughout the operation, not to disturb the rubble inside the chamber because it might damage the contents.

Callender and Mace helped Carter to make a small opening.

"I had to resist, at every moment, the temptation of stopping to look inside," wrote Carter.

At last, after a few moments, the gap was large enough for Carter to pass through an electric lamp.

What he saw filled him with amazement: the beam of his lamp revealed a wall of gold . . .

"This time, we are really first!"

The officials and experts were then invited by Carter to witness this fabulous sight.

"We could," wrote Carter, "as though by electric current, feel the tingle of excitement which thrilled the spectators behind the barrier."

After two hours of laborious and painstaking efforts, the hole was large enough for a man to climb through. Carter did so carefully, and noticed that the level of this new chamber was about four feet lower than that of the antechamber. He estimated that it was some 14 feet wide and 20 feet long.

Carter then realized that the expanse of gold which he had taken to be a wall, was in fact the side of a huge gilded wooden shrine, which almost filled the entire room. A small gap of about 2 feet separated the shrine from the walls of the chamber, and Carter had to proceed with extreme caution, because the floor of this chamber too was littered with funerary offerings.

"Our presence there seemed to be a sacrilege," he wrote.

On one side of the shrine Carter discovered double doors which were fastened but not sealed. Had the mummy been stripped, destroyed or stolen?

Steadying his shaking hands as best he could, Carter drew back the ebony latch. To his great surprise, a second shrine could be seen. Carnarvon and Lacau, who had joined Carter, heaved a sigh of relief. The clay seal covering the latch of this second shrine was still intact. It bore two different imprints: that of the royal necropolis, and that of Tutankhamen.

"This time, we are first!" exclaimed Carter. "The robbers have never seen this shrine."

"I think we are first," added Carnarvon, who found it hard to control his emotion.

FOUR SHRINES
AND THREE COFFINS

WHILE the three archeologists were leaving the burial chamber, Carter discovered a small opening in the northeastern corner of the room.

This last chamber, 14 feet by 11 feet, was completely plain. But they realized, at a glance, that it contained the most precious objects in the whole tomb.

Carter immediately named this room "The Treasury."

A breathtaking sight

The robbers had clearly penetrated as far as the burial chamber. The contents of most of the shrines (approximately 60 % according to the experts) had been stolen. But the robbers clearly did not have time to take everything.

Apart from the valuable items, they found in one of the many coffers a dressing-case, and in another a scribe's materials, including two ivory palettes, a wooden bowl, two blocks of color, an ivory papyrus "smoother," and a strange little box containing pens like those used until recently in school.

Other chests contained medicines. There was also the model of a granary and a hand-mill to grind the corn, two beer filters, leather sandals, stone anklets, various strange objects the purpose of which escaped the archeologists, and much more beside.

Amazed and delighted beyond their wildest dreams, Carter, Carnarvon and Lacau went back to the antechamber. They needed to make preparations for protecting the mummy.

The death of Lord Carnarvon

These preparations took several months.

The entrance to the tomb, blocked once more as a security measure, was guarded by teams of armed guards.

The day after the discovery, Lord Carnarvon returned to Cairo.

At the start of April, 1923, Carter received at Luxor—where he was staying—a message informing him that Lord Carnarvon was sick. Convinced that this was a simple attack of fever, so common in the Orient, Carter was not unduly alarmed.

A few days later, a second telegram informed him: "Lord Carnarvon seriously ill." Alarmed by this, he set off at once for Cairo.

Shortly afterwards, Carter witnessed the death of his patron, friend and companion. They had shared some of the most difficult, most incredible moments that any archeologist would be likely to experience.

After the funeral, Carter returned alone to resume the task of opening the coffins.

Three weeks' work

Firstly, a team of skilled workmen hired by Carter, proceeded to dismantle the outer shrine.

It was built of planks nearly two inches thick. The wood had dried out during the centuries, and the stucco which covered it was cracked and might fall away at any moment.

The immense weight of the side-panels made the workmen's task even more difficult.

At last, after several days of laborious effort, the shrine was completely dismantled.

They now had to remove the linen pall which covered the second coffin without causing any damage. For this reason, the fabric was soaked in a special solution to make it less fragile and allow it to be moved.

After more than three weeks' work, the first three shrines were ready to be transferred to the Cairo Museum.

A fascinating effigy

Inside the last shrine was a sarcophagus of yellow quartzite, 9 feet in length, 4 feet 10 inches wide and 4 feet 10 inches high, and covered by a huge slab of rose granite.

On February 3, 1924, in the presence of several eminent people, the lid was raised by means of winches. Inside, Carter found a mummiform coffin covered by several linen shrouds blackened by age. Patiently, delicately, the archeologists removed them one at a time until the fascinating effigy of the young Pharaoh was finally revealed.

The enthusiasm aroused by this unforgettable discovery was dampened the next day by a strange decision from the authorities in Cairo.

The Egyptians forbid women to visit the tomb of Tutankhamen

On February 4, Carter received a telegram from the Egyptian Government forbidding women to visit the tomb, which had just been opened to the public.

Concerning this strange affair, and the quarrel between Carter and the Egyptians, we have the testimony of one of Carter's former colleagues, the young Austrian architect Otto Neubert.

"Carter and his team," he wrote in his memoirs *The Valley of the Kings,* "considered this ban an act of provocation, and they protested by threatening to stop work. Carter had the tomb closed, but without replacing the lid of the sarcophagus, thinking that the incident would be forgotten in a few days. He asked the Egyptian Government to appoint him Curator of the Tomb; but they forbade him to enter it, and when he asked permission to return in order to replace the lid, the Egyptians accused him of negligence and withdrew his concession.

Howard Carter and his assistants are shown here in the antechambre of the tomb of Tutankhamen. They are wrapping the statues which guarded the threshold of the burial chamber. Carter, the Englishman, was the initiator of "the greatest discovery in the Valley of the Kings." The "chief violator" of this magnificent pharaonic tomb did not succumb to the "curse" for he died 17 years later in 1939. "Of his companions, the 'discoverers,' 23 died under more or less strange circumstances." *L'Illustration, Ferni.*

"Carter had been living in Egypt for thirty years. He had discovered the tomb of Thutmose IV and had recently been appointed Inspector-in-chief of Antiquities in Upper Egypt. He had devoted many years and the greater part of his work to the discovery of Tutankhamen's tomb.

"Thousands of tourists had flocked in, bringing great benefits to Egypt. Carter, as a true scientist, had sacrificed his own health and neglected his personal interests. He had even quarrelled with his friend Carnarvon, insisting that the treasures should remain the property of the Egyptian Government.

"After having done so much good for the country he loved, he was prevented from carrying on his work."

Carter the victim of the Anglo-Egyptian crisis

One morning, as Carter was still refusing to hand over the keys of the tomb, a government representative, accompanied by several lawyers and locksmiths, arrived on the scene.

New locks were fitted, the lid of the sarcophagus was replaced and an armed guard was posted around the tomb.

Carter was desperate : thirty years of sacrifice could not be wiped out in a single day!

He hired a famous lawyer to defend his interests. Messages of support flooded in from around the world, and American archeologists offered to mediate.

But Carter was British, and relations between Britain and Egypt were bad at the time. Although Egypt had been independent since

February 21, 1922, her sovereignty was limited. Britain reserved the right to protect communications with the British Empire and maintained certain military prerogatives. Egyptian Nationalists were opposed to this "occupation in disguise" and fought it, led by Zaglul and the *Wafd* party.

The 1924 elections had just put the Nationalists in power. They were exasperated by the British "occupation," and in their eyes Carter and his compatriots incarnated British imperialism.

Convinced that he had been unjustly treated, Carter decided to return to England.

He did not return to resume his work until the winter of 1925, when the political situation had more or less calmed down.

2,500 pounds of solid gold

It was not until October 10, 1925, that the first coffin was opened.

A second, smaller coffin fitted perfectly inside the first; so perfectly, in fact, that it was not possible to insert a hand between them. Like the first, it was made of wood covered in gold leaf.

But why was it so heavy? Was the inner coffin made of lead? When, on October 28, Carter approached the second coffin, he was not expecting the shock which awaited him. With the help of his assistants, Carter grabbed one of the silver handles on the lid and lifted it.

A red shroud was visible, covering the king's body. Only the face was uncovered, and was, in fact, a solid gold mask incrusted with precious stones.

Carter began to remove the shroud. As the legs and the body of the Pharaoh were gradually revealed, all those present were taken aback. The coffin was made entirely of solid gold——the finest example of a goldsmith's art ever uncovered.

The coffin was six feet long and almost a quarter of an inch thick in places. About 2,500 pounds of solid gold in all.

"What condition will the mummy be in?"

As soon as he recovered from his initial surprise, Carter voiced the question which he had been asking himself since he opened the second coffin.

"What condition will the mummy be in?" he asked his assistant Dr. Lucas. "Will the humidity and the pomades have damaged it?"

"I think it would be best to analyze the pomades before we proceed."

This suggestion was adopted, and analysis revealed that they were composed of resin and an unidentified fatty substance. This conclusion was confirmed when they tried to open the coffin.

The pitch had solidified and made the process of separation extremely difficult.

After several attempts, the archeologists managed to perfect a system. It needed weeks of effort in the heat and darkness of this tiny room, where the thermometer often read up to 113° Fahrenheit for the supreme objective to be achieved. Tutankhamen, the boy king of Thebes, at last revealed his face.

Chapter V

AUTOPSY
OF THE ROYAL MUMMY

O N November 11, 1925, at about 9.45, a strange event took place at the Institute of Anatomy in the University of Cairo. The body on the autopsy table was none other than Tutankhamen.

A strange dissection

When Dr. Douglas Derry placed his instruments beside the mummy, anxiety seized the group of eminent people invited to witness this strange dissection. From Saleh Enan Pacha, Under-Secretary of State at the Egyptian Ministry of Public Affairs, to Said Fuad Bey el Kholi, Governor of the Province of Kena, Pierre Lacau, Dr. Saleh Bey Hamdi, Director of the Public Health Department of Alexandria, Alfred Lucas, Harry Burton, Texsik Effen di Boulos, Chief Inspector of the Antiquities Department of Upper

Egypt, Muhamed Chaaban Effendi, one of the Curators of the Cairo Museum—all these people felt that this was some sort of sacrilege.

A scalpel is used for the autopsy

Dr. Derry covered the whole body in paraffin wax to preserve the bandages. Then he made the first incision, from the chest to the toes.

It was not a deep incision. Derry was trying to release the body from its covering of bandages.

As the autopsy proceeded, Derry encountered several problems. The bands of material—from two to four inches wide—had been wrapped around the body up to sixteen times in places. The pomades had hardened to such an extent that a scalpel had to be used to separate the layers of material. Between each layer Derry found precious objects wrapped in little canvas bags and obviously intended to preserve the appearance of the mummy.

The Pharaoh's skin had literally been carbonized by the pomades

While the audience gazed in amazement at these treasures, Derry continued his work.

The closer he got to the body, the more the bandages disintegrated. When the final stage was reached, Derry observed that the arms, legs and penis had been separated from the body. The head had been swathed in bandages. A pad in the form of a crown protected the face from the weight of the mask.

Then came the moment when Derry removed the last bandage from the top of the legs. Visitors and experts alike could not conceal their disappointment.

The skin was gray, hard and wrinkled. It had literally been carbonized by the pomades.

The realism of the Egyptian artists

Had the gold mask prevented a similar deterioration of the face? This was the hope of all those present as Derry began to remove the bandages from the King's head.

This was, naturally, the most delicate part of the whole operation.

As the bandages were removed, the familiar shape of Tutankhamen's skull emerged. Thanks to the frescoes and statues found in the tomb, it was clear that the back of the skull was exceptionally prominent. The information contained in such works of art was extremely detailed, for the artists of the time made every effort to reproduce accurately and with vivid realism the features of a person or the shape of an object.

The magic power of the diadem

After removing a few more inches of bandage, Derry discovered the diadem.

It was of gold, decorated with cornelian, and fitted the head perfectly.

By studying two objects found beside the king's legs a few days later, the experts arrived at an interesting conclusion: the diadem had originally been decorated with two objects. These two emblems, a vulture and a cobra, the symbols of Lower and Upper Egypt respectively, had joints which fitted exactly the holes in the front of the diadem.

Diadems possessed—in the eyes of the Ancient Egyptians—a certain magical power. On a papyrus belonging to the Russian collector Vladimir Golenisheff, usually referred to as the *Diadem Papyrus,* an interesting text is to be found. "The awesome diadem which shines on the foreheads of the sun-god and the earthly kings and overcomes their enemies."

"The peaceful and gentle face of the young man"

Dr. Derry removed a few more layers and found a linen cap covered in pearls and small pieces of gold.

This was the final stage. When this thin layer was removed, the face of Tutankhamen would appear...

Derry picked up a small sable brush and began to clean the surface of the head. Gradually, with delicate strokes, he removed the particles of material.

One hour later "the peaceful and gentle face of the young man" was completely uncovered.

The pomades had unfortunately caused some damage. But the king's features were intact.

The eyelids, which were slightly opened, had long, curved lashes, and revealed the dried eyeballs of the corpse.

The nose was slightly flattened, and the nostrils (through which the brain had been removed) were blocked with small plugs of resin.

Only the teeth seemed to have suffered no damage. Long incisors protruded from the lips.

The ears were small and had been pierced, for Tutankhamen ——like all the Pharaohs, wore large earrings.

How old was the king?

The first and most striking thing was the extreme youth of the face. What was the exact age of the king when he died?

During the days which followed, Derry tried to answer this question by analyzing the king's bone structure. Osteology makes it possible to determine the age of a body.

Derry studied first the knee joint. Around the age of 20, the cartilage adheres to the femur. This had not yet happened to Tutankhamen.

On the other hand, another cartilage, which usually adheres around the age of 18 had done so in the case of the king.

Thus Tutankhamen would have died between the ages of 18 and 20. This approximation was not good enough for the doctor, who proceeded to examine the two bones of the forearm to obtain some confirmation, and, if possible, some more conclusive evidence.

By using X rays, Derry revealed that the inner part of the cubitus had begun to adhere to the radius.

Derry knew that, in Orientals, this process took place at the age of 18, earlier than in Europeans.

This seemed to prove conclusively that Tutankhamen had died at the age of 18.

Some amazingly detailed conclusions

While Dr. Derry was at work, other experts carried out their own detailed study of the objects found in the tomb of Tutankhamen.

One such was Alfred Lucas, who was later to produce in a book entitled *The Chemistry of the Tombs* his conclusions concerning the metals, oils, fats and textiles.

Professor Alphonse Alfieri, entomologist of the Royal Egyptian Society of Agriculture, examined the insects found in the tomb.

Among all these studies, too numerous to be mentioned here, there was one which unexpectedly complemented the work of Dr. Derry. It was the research of the scientist P.G. Newberry.

He analyzed the flowers found near the body. There were rare plants, like the wreaths of wild celery, or more common varieties, like olive leaves, or the cornflowers which grew in such profusion in the cornfields along the banks of the Nile. There were also lotus and papyrus, the two symbols of the Egypt of the Pharaohs. Newberry was also interested in the fruits. One, in particular, attracted his attention: the mandrake, or "tuffah el djinn" (the devil's apple) as the Arabs called it. When taken in small quantities, it possessed aphrodisiac properties, and in large quantities, it caused madness.

Newberry was unable to determine the origin of this fruit. But in trying to detect it, he reached some interesting conclusions.

Three thousand years and more after the burial of the body, he was able to tell accurately the season when Tutankhamen had died.

By comparing the ripeness of the mandrake and the growth of the many plants found in the tomb, he was able to conclude that the burial must have taken place between mid-March and the end of April.

X rays reveal that Tutankhamen died a violent death

What was the cause of Tutankhamen's premature demise? Sickness, cancer, accident or assassination?

A wound on the king's left cheek, to which nobody paid much attention, was to provide the answer.

In his account of the autopsy, Derry simply noted: "It is impossible to ascertain the cause of this wound."

It was necessary to wait for forty years, until Dr. Ronald Harrison, Professor of Anatomy at the University of Liverpool, proved conclusively that Tutankhamen had been assassinated.

Harrison used X rays in his analysis, which took place in the tomb of Tutankhamen itself.

A highly sophisticated portable machine was used, and the 50 plates taken proved that the cause of the king's death was a blood clot beneath the cerebral cortex caused by a violent blow.

The king's height is measured

The research of the English expert Karl Pearson was perhaps the most precise of all the efforts we have mentioned.

Pearson established the exact height of the king when he was alive, to the nearest fraction of an inch.

Just as Derry had done, Pearson examined the bones; but he was not concerned with the state of the cartilages, rather in the length of the bones themselves.

By tabulating the size of the skeleton in this way, he was able to conclude that Tutankhamen was 1.676 meter tall.

This estimate is confirmed by the measurements of the two statues guarding the entrance to the burial chamber.

Thanks to such close co-operation between specialists of all nationalities on a wide variety of subjects, often unconnected with archeology, they were able to create with incredible accuracy a picture of the youngest Pharaoh of the 18th Dynasty.

PART THREE

THE SUCCESSION OF CURSES

*"The Kings of Egypt protected their tombs
by secret methods which were so effective that,
even after several centuries, those who defied
them by plundering the tombs suffered
their terrible effects."*

J.C. Mardrus

Chapter 1

SOME STRANGE DEATHS

SCEPTICS will say, with Howard Carter, that all the stories of the vengeance of the Pharaohs are merely a "poor sort of ghost story."

There are many, however, who remain convinced that the curses pronounced three thousand years ago by the Ancient Egyptians continue to exercise their evil influence.

The list of people who have died after direct or indirect contact with the tombs or the mummies of the Pharaohs is surprising. In less than 50 years, there have been about 40 "strange deaths."

What are the apparent causes? In certain cases, the victim suffered a violent attack of fever leading to delirium. Others were the victims of cancer, but the most frequent cause seems to be a heart attack.

Certain Egyptologists have suffered paralysis, nervous depression or mental disorders.

Lord Carnarvon: "I am not feeling at all well"

The story of the "curse of the Pharaohs" was given prominence by the sudden death of Lord Carnarvon in April 1923, just a few weeks after the discovery of Tutankhamen's tomb.

Six weeks before his death Lord Carnarvon went to the Valley of the Kings, as he had done every day, to follow the progress of the excavations.

For some time he had a dressing on his cheek, because he had been stung by a mosquito while shaving, and the bite had not healed.

"I am not feeling at all well these days," Carnarvon confided to Carter. "I must see a doctor."

He felt extremely weak. Nausea and giddiness became more and more frequent. And he could no longer stand the bright sunlight to which he had grown accustomed after almost 17 years in Egypt.

Moslem pilgrims pray for Lord Carnarvon

On March 27, 1923, Lord Carnarvon collapsed in the tomb of Tutankhamen. He was taken immediately to his apartment in Cairo, where he became delirious.

The doctor diagnosed congestion of the lungs.

The condition of the patient deteriorated daily. He suffered dreadful nightmares. His temperature rose and fell.

His son, Lord Porchester, an officer in the Indian Army, learned the sad news. He tried to get to his father's bedside as quickly as possible.

A funeral bed found in the antechamber to Tutankhamen's tomb. This mobile bed of plaster-covered wood, decorated with bronze and black stars, was most likely the table on which the rites and operations of mummification had taken place. Shaped like a cow, it represents the goddess Hator or Isis-Mehet. Her task was to receive the deceased in the other world. *Ferri*.

The name of Lord Carnarvon was known throughout the world since the discovery of the tomb. His son had no difficulty in getting a passage on a boat bound for Egypt.

During the voyage, Lord Porchester witnessed a strange occurrence: some Moslem pilgrims who had learned the news prayed night and day to Allah and his Prophet to save the life of Lord Carnarvon.

"I have heard the call of Tutankhamen," said Lord Carnarvon before he died

Lord Porchester reached Cairo on April 4, 1923, just a few hours before his father died.

"When I reached Cairo," he relates, "I went immediately to the Hotel Continental. My father was unconscious. Howard Carter was there, and Lady Almina, my mother. In the night, I was awakened at ten minutes to two precisely. The nurse told me that my father was dead, and that my mother, who had stayed at his bedside, had closed his eyes. When I entered the room, the lights suddenly went out, and we had to light candles. After three minutes, the lights came back on. I held my father's hand and started to pray."

Lady Burghclere, Lord Carnarvon's sister, and also present at his bedside, notes in her memoirs that the archeologist's last words were: "I have heard the call of Tutankhamen... I am going to follow him."

The mysterious power cut

Lord Porchester was intrigued by the fact that the lights had gone out at the precise moment that his father had died.

The next day, when he went to the Residence of the Governor, Lord Allenby, to complete the formalities, he learned that the Hotel Continental was not the only building plunged into darkness that night; all the lights in the city had gone out.

At the request of Lord Allenby, an investigation was carried out at the main power station.

"There is no technical explanation," said the experts.

Lord Porchester, now sixth Earl of Carnarvon, relates another interesting fact: "My father died shortly before 2a.m. (Cairo time). I learned later that a strange event had occurred on the family estate at Highclere, just before midnight (London time)—in other words, at the same time as my father was dying. Our fox-terrier bitch, who had lost her left front paw as the result of an accident in 1919, and who was my father's favorite, suddenly started to whine, stood up on her hind legs and fell down dead."

A whole series of inexplicable deaths

These events caused the Press to talk of strange happenings, surprising coincidences and an invisible power—or, in other words, the curse of the Pharaohs.

It is true that the succession of deaths in the years which followed lent credibility to such theories.

For several years, death struck down not only members of the excavation team itself, but also those connected in some way with the project, visitors to the tomb or simply relatives and friends of the archeologists.

"I am a victim of the Curse"

The Canadian archeologist La Fleur arrived in Egypt in April 1923 in perfect health. A close friend of Carter, whom he had come to assist, La Fleur was struck down by a mysterious illness just a few weeks after his arrival.

The third victim was the English archeologist Arthur C. Mace, who had helped Carter to remove the door of the burial chamber. Soon after Lord Carnarvon's death, he was filled with anxiety. His strength gradually ebbed away, until he finally lost consciousness and died—in the same hotel as Lord Carnarvon—without any apparent cause.

Next came the turn of the American millionaire George Jay Gould, one of the oldest acquaintances of Lord Carnarvon, who had come to Egypt to pay his last respects to his friend. Fascinated by the work being carried out in the Valley of the Kings, he asked Carter to let him see the tomb. The day after his visit, Jay Gould suffered a violent attack of fever and died the same evening.

Dr. Evelyn White, a famous archeologist, and colleague of Carter, hanged himself shortly afterwards. Feeling uneasy every time he had to enter the burial chamber, he finally fell prey to nervous depression, which drove him to suicide.

In his farewell note he wrote: "I am a victim of the Curse, which has forced me to take my life."

A lethal hearse

Alfred Lucas and Douglas Derry were to die in their turn. Archeologists throughout the world began to panic.

The two experts had been present at the autopsy of Tutankhamen, and both died shortly afterwards of heart attacks.

Soon after this, the half-brother of Lord Carnarvon, Aubrey Herbert, committed suicide as the result of a sudden and inexplicable fit of madness.

In February 1929, Lady Almina, the wife of Lord Carnarvon, died in strange circumstances. An insect bite, according to the doctors, was the cause of her sudden death.

During that same fateful year of 1929, in the month of November, Richard Bethell, Carter's former secretary, was found dead in bed. Heart failure, said the doctors.

Richard Bethell was the only son of Lord Westbury. Three months later, at the age of 78, he too committed suicide by jumping from the window of his seventh-floor London apartment.

During his funeral, the hearse overran two youths. One of them died on the way to the hospital.

The 27th victim of Tutankhamen

England was just recovering from the news of these two deaths when a new scare began, as is made clear by the newspapers of the time.

Archibald Douglas Reed, an English scientist on loan to the Egyptian Government, also died. He had received instructions a few days earlier to X-ray the mummy of Tutankhamen. His task was to detect any foreign bodies which might lie inside the corpse.

After the X-ray session, he felt unwell. A few days later he died, although he had never previously had a day's illness in his life.

A few weeks later, Arthur Weigall, the famous historian of Ancient Egypt, fell victim to a strange fever.

Just as strange was the illness which killed Herbert Winlock, the eminent Egyptologist attached to the New York Museum. In December 1935, twelve years after the discovery of the tomb, the Beirut daily *L'Orient-Le Jour,* which kept a detailed record of all the deaths caused by the Curse, announced the death of the 27th victim.

"Since the mysterious death of Lord Carnarvon, Tutankhamen has claimed twenty-seven victims from the people involved in the discovery of his tomb. The latest death is that of Mr. James Breasted, of the University of Chicago."

Laboratory investigation produces no explanation

James Henry Breasted was one of the archeologists who, with Carter, had spent the longest time in the tomb.

His son Charles, who accompanied him on his travels, described in his memoirs the strange illness which attacked his father. "Every night the fever returned. He had pains in his throat, started to shiver, and felt at certain moments that his blood was boiling in his veins, and that his head was bursting. He assumed that this was the return of the malaria that he had contracted in Mesopotamia. But the English doctor who was treating him could find no clue as to the nature of the ailment, and the quinine prescribed for him gave him no relief."

Eighteen months before the death of Breasted, his wife, who had followed her husband on all his expeditions, also died. "She grew more and more tired," wrote Charles, "until she finally fell into a coma from which she was never to awaken."

Remember the tablet! say the "fellahs"

In the meantime, ten other archeologists met their deaths. Professors Sir Alan Gardiner and Fouchard, the archeologist Davies, who had found the famous goblet bearing the name of Tutankhamen, Harkness, the well-known Egyptologist, the assistants Astor and Callender, the scientists Bruyère and Bethell, the researcher Joel Woolf, and the Chief Curator of Egyptian Antiquities at the Louvre, Georges Bénédite, who died after visiting the tomb . . .

These ten victims, like the seventeen others we have mentioned, all died under strange circumstances.

The *fellahs*, however, did not find this at all strange. Only the curse of the Pharaohs could explain these events.

"Remember," they said, "the inscription found on the tablet in the antechamber: 'Death will slay with his wings whoever disturbs the peace of the Pharaoh.'"

Carter's canary eaten by a cobra

The curse seemed to affect birds too. The German archeologist Otto Neubert tells a story about Carter in his memoirs.

"He had spent many years in Egypt and lived only for archeology. Never having had time to start a family, when he went back to England for a brief visit he said to everybody: 'I'm tired of living alone.' Was he intending to get married? Was he perhaps already engaged? Carter soon provided the answer: he bought a canary!

"The natives, believing that this bird brought good luck, called the tomb the 'Tomb of the Bird.' They also believed that the two statues found in the antechamber, which had on their headdress the sacred snake symbolizing the king's protective spirit, would slay his enemies at all times.

"A strange event soon took place. The bird's cage stood in front of Carter's hut, on a pile of rocks. As usual, the bird was singing merrily. When Carter's valet approached to investigate a sudden silence, a terrifying spectacle awaited him. A huge cobra was in front of the cage busy devouring the poor bird. The natives mentioned the Curse once more, and warned the Europeans of the risk they ran."

CHAPTER II

THE CURSE OF TUTANKHAMEN, OR THE CURSE OF THE PHARAOHS?

ALL these deaths were connected in some way with the discovery of Tutankhamen's tomb.

But it is interesting to note that many Egyptologists had died long before 1923, when the tomb was first opened.

Just as unusual are the more recent deaths of other archeologists who were investigating other Pharaohs.

Which leads us to ask the question: is the curse—if it exists—only connected with the tomb of Tutankhamen, or is it more general, striking all those who, during their investigations, disturb the eternal peace of the Pharaohs? Belzoni, Bilharz, Brugsch, Goneim and many others, were they all victims of the curse?

When he first arrived in Egypt in 1815 with his wife and an Irish servant, Giovanni Battista Belzoni, from Padua in Italy, had no idea that one day he would discover the tomb of the Pharaoh Seti I.

The incredible Belzoni had begun his chequered career by inventing a water-wheel "four times as efficient as conventional waterwheels." Then he traveled around the world, to England, Portugal and Africa, doing a variety of things: circus performer, strongman, actor and even opera singer...

When he arrived in Egypt, Belzoni demonstrated the water-wheel to the Sultan Mohammed Ali, who was not impressed and declined the offer of the patent. Belzoni was not discouraged, and, since he liked the country, decided to stay on. What could he do in Egypt except archeology? Belzoni, the jack-of-all-trades, did not hesitate for a moment.

"To make a fortune off the Pharaohs" (Belzoni)

For several years, the incredible Belzoni explored with great energy the necropolis at Thebes.

For the first two years, his primary motive was to make a lot of money.

Since Napoleon's expedition to Egypt, Egyptian antiquities were greatly sought after in Europe, and sold readily. Belzoni decided, as he himself admitted, to make a fortune "off the Pharaohs."

His *Narrative of the Operations and Recent Discoveries in Egypt and Nubia* includes several amusing episodes which occurred during his investigations.

"One day," he wrote, "I discovered a passage of about twenty feet in length, only just wide enough for a body to be forced through. It was choked with mummies, and I could not pass without putting my face in contact with that of some decayed Egyptian;

but as the passage inclined downwards, my own weight helped me on: however, I could not help being covered with bones, legs, arms and heads rolling from above. Thus I proceeded from one cave to another, all full of mummies piled up in various ways, some standing, some lying, and some on their heads."

The underground chamber of Cheops was empty

Belzoni finally became genuinely fascinated by his new profession. Gradually the money-grabbing tomb robber became a genuine archeologist.

In 1817 he discovered the tomb of Seti I, fully excavated it, recorded the inscriptions, made moulds and drawings and, in the process——to the dismay of his wife——swallowed up most of his savings. "The discovery of this tomb," wrote Belzoni in his diary, "rewarded me for all the efforts I had put into my research. This was possibly the finest day in my whole life."

Shortly after this discovery, he learned that one of his compatriots, Captain Caviglia, was busy excavating the shaft inside the pyramid of Cheops. With the aid of his friend Salt, the British Consul in Alexandria, Belzoni joined Caviglia's team and involved himself with the work. Several inner galleries were cleared and the underground chamber was reached. But it was empty, and the walls bore only a few Greek and Roman graffiti.

Belzoni is not afraid of ridicule

Belzoni's enthusiasm was in no way dampened by this setback.

"Why," he said to Caviglia one day, "concentrate on the pyramid of Cheops? There are many other monuments worth investigating."

The amateur archeologist rightly believed that greater rewards were in store for those who would explore the other pyramids. He decided to turn his attention to the pyramid of Chephren.

Where was the entrance to this monument? Many archeologists, including Caviglia, had looked for it in vain. "Tormented by this idea," wrote Belzoni, "I started to examine the southern face." He made a minute examination of the base, studying each crack and irregularity. On the northern face, the traditional site of the entrances to tombs, he found three marks. "If I fail," he said, "I shall expose myself to public ridicule." But he had the audacity of the true amateur. After making approaches to the Cachef of Embabeh and the Pacha of Cairo, he arrived at the pyramid with a small tent and £ 200 in his pocket.

The Pyramids are tombs

Near the eastern face, Belzoni noticed traces of a temple, with a path leading in a straight line towards the Sphinx. He set his team of 40 Arabs to work between the temple and the pyramid to find an entrance of some sort. The workmen toiled for several weeks.

Finally, on February 18, 1818, one of them noticed a gap between two stones and inserted a long wooden pole.

Encouraged by this find, Belzoni continued his exploration and finally entered the pyramid of Chephren in April 1818. In the burial chamber he discovered a sarcophagus with a broken lid. This was an important discovery, since the archeologists of the day were not sure whether the Pyramids were in fact tombs. Added to the other finds, the sarcophagus in the pyramid of Chephren strengthened the arguments of of those who believed this to be the case, as most Egyptologists now admit.

Commenting on this discovery, Belzoni wrote: "Since it contains chambers and a sarcophagus destined in all probability for some great personage, there can be little doubt that it was used as a tomb, and I do not see how this can be disputed... The desire to discover something new has given rise to the most bizarre suppositions, and it seems that much effort has been expended to ignore what was so obvious to the eyes and the mind. Perhaps if the ancients had said that the Egyptians had built the pyramids as store-houses for their treasures, the moderns would have proved scientifically that the pyramids were only tombs, and then all the evidence which supports the truth would have been given due weight."

"I feel the hand of death upon me!"

After this brilliant success, Belzoni abandoned archeology for the time being to embark on another adventure.

Fascinated by the unexplored regions of Africa, Belzoni proposed to try and answer the question—much debated at the time: were the Nile and the Niger the same river, with no source and two mouths? To determine this, he would have to travel to West Africa. Since the expedition would be costly, the ingenious Belzoni went to England taking several antiquities with him, including the sarcophagus of Seti I. In April 1823, he organised an exhibition in London, made some money and embarked with his wife for Tangiers. From there he hoped to reach the Sudan by crossing the Sahara. A few days after leaving Tangiers, Belzoni was turned back by Tuaregs. He then decided to travel to Sierra Leone by boat.

There he was seized by a raging fever and became delirious. "I feel the hand of death upon me... I know that I have only a few hours to live."

An African witch-doctor gave him opium to calm the fever, but in vain. On December 3, 1823, Belzoni died, cursing Seti I in his delirium.

"The Pharaohs have had their revenge," said the witch-doctor.

A mysterious fever kills Theodor Bilharz

Thirty-nine years later, in 1862, a German doctor and researcher, Theodor Bilharz, died under similar circumstances.

Qualified as a doctor at the age of 25, Bilharz had a practice in Tübingen with another doctor, Wilhelm Griesinger.

When the latter was asked by the Viceroy of Egypt to take up an appointment in that country, Bilharz accompanied him as his assistant. When, shortly afterwards, Griesinger resigned, Bilharz replaced him.

Fascinated by archeology, Bilharz rapidly specialized in the autopsy of mummies.

His talent as a linguist enabled him to act as interpreter for the many teams of archeologists. He was also entrusted by the Egyptian Government with the task of conducting eminent visitors around the principal sites.

In the summer of 1862, while he was showing Luxor to one of these visitors, he started to shiver. Taken to the house of one of his friends, Professor Lautner, Bilharz remained delirious for a fortnight, then died without having regained consciousness. The cause of his illness was never determined.

Lautner, who witnessed the last moments of Bilharz, declared that "a mysterious and unknown fever" had carried off his friend.

The ingenious theory of Lepsius concerning the construction of the pyramids

Richard Lepsius was to live to the ripe age of 74, but he was half paralyzed for many years.

A professor at the University of Berlin, and a well-known philologist and grammarian, Lepsius took charge—at the age of 31—of an expedition sponsored by Frederick-William IV of Prussia.

This expedition lasted from the autumn of 1842 to the end of 1845. When he returned to Berlin in 1846 he began to publish the mass of drawings and prints which he had collected during his excavations. The first of twelve volumes appeared in 1849, and the last some seven years later in 1856. The majority of the plates were devoted to inscriptions and bas-reliefs, but the first two volumes contained maps and views of the sites and monuments. As far as the pyramids were concerned, Lepsius published a plan of the Memphis burial ground in several plates. It remains today an excellent document.

Apart from this plan, Lepsius only included pictures of the outside of the pyramids. But in his diary he included brief comments on most of the pyramids.

After having studied the internal structure of the great pyramid of Abu Sir, the pyramid of Meidum and the step-pyramid of Sakkara, he suggested that all, or almost all the pyramids—including those at Gizeh, had been built in tiers, with the later additions of layers of masonry.

Basing his conclusions on this hypothesis, he enunciated his famous theory. Each king had added to his pyramid throughout his reign. The dimensions of any pyramid were in direct proportion to the length of the Pharaoh's reign, and the length of the reign could be determined by the number of successive layers, just as the age of a tree is determined by the number of rings in its trunk.

The invisible hand of the Pharaohs

Such was, in brief, the career of the great Egyptologist Lepsius. Victim of a heart attack in his later years, he remained partly paralyzed and died in 1884. The doctors diagnosed cancer. This did

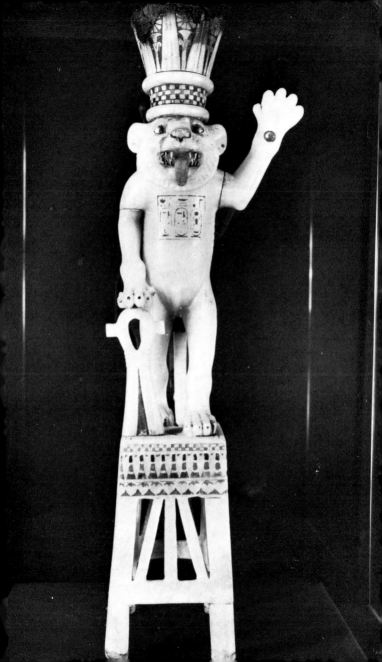

The pomade vessel illustrated here, was made of alabaster and inlaid with gold and ivory. It shows a grimacing lion representing the god Mahes. His task was to provide the unguents which were indispensable for the rites of rebirth. Its posture is highly symbolic: it is the one of a terrible and threatening guardian. *The Cairo Museum, Femi.*

not prevent a German journalist from claiming that Lepsius had been struck by the "invisible hand" of the Pharaohs. "The sacred land of Egypt cannot be excavated with impunity," he wrote. "The statues and mummies of the Pharaohs cannot be removed to enrich the Berlin Museum. These are acts of sacrilege which must be paid for, sooner or later, with the life of the archeologist."

Symptoms of madness

The same "invisible hand" does not seem to have spared another Berlin archeologist, Heinrich Brugsch.

He lived for many years in Egypt and was fascinated by the ancient history of the country.

Two of his books earned him a special reputation: his *Geography of Ancient Egypt* and *History of Egypt under the Pharaohs*.

Despite his great work, Brugsch showed signs of mental disturbance throughout his life.

Gaston Maspero affirmed that, in one of his books, Brugsch had quoted documents of his own invention.

These symptoms of madness, so common to those stricken by the curse of the Pharaohs, grew worse when Brugsch returned to Berlin.

On the slightest of pretexts he would attack certain German newspapers and accuse them of showing insufficient interest in his work. He claimed to be the victim of a plot, and declared that the world of archeology was afraid of the "terrible revelations" which he was in a position to make.

Confined to a psychiatric clinic in Berlin, Heinrich Brugsch died in 1907, after terrible attacks of madness.

A live broadcast from the Great Pyramid

Through these four examples taken from the 19th century, we can see that the main causes of death were heart attacks, fever accompanied by delirium, cancer and madness.

In the 20th century too, the deaths of many archeologists were caused in the same way.

In 1942, for example, the sudden death of the American archeologist George A. Reisner was announced.

Between 1920 and 1930, Reisner had made some great discoveries, like the tomb of Queen Hetepheres, whose pyramid was close to that of Cheops. But above all he was known as the producer of a famous radio broadcast in 1939.

He organized a live broadcast from inside the royal chamber of the Pyramid of Cheops. In the spring of 1942, while working inside the pyramid, Reisner collapsed as the result of a heart attack. Taken back to his tent, he died without having regained consciousness.

Emery "fascinated" by the statue of Osiris

Just as sudden were the deaths of Dr. Zakaria Goneim and the English archeologist, Walter Bryan Emery.

The former was Chief Inspector of the Administration of

Antiquities in Upper Egypt, which involved him in many visits to the tombs of the Pharaohs. After having complained for many years of severe nervous trouble, Goneim, in a fit of madness, killed himself in 1959 by jumping into the Nile.

Emery was a professor of Egyptology, and, from 1835, he directed operations at Sakkara. This large field, about 20 miles south of Cairo, was the ancient necropolis of Memphis, which is overlooked by the impressive step-pyramid of King Djoser.

Starting in 1964, Emery tried, in common with several others, to find the tomb of Imhotep.

On March 10, 1971, while Emery's workmen were removing a mass of sand and rubble, a small statuette about seven inches high appeared. Emery grabbed hold of it and "stared at it in fascination" according to those present at the time. It was an image of Osiris.

At siesta time, Emery and his assistant Ali el Khuli went back to the hut where they rested in the afternoons.

"The curse of the Pharaohs has struck again"

Emery went to the bathroom to freshen up while the exhausted Ali slumped onto the divan and began to doze. "Suddenly," he relates, "I heard Emery groan in the bathroom. I got up and saw him, through the half-open door, obviously in great pain, gripping the wash basin. I shouted 'Are you ill?' But he did not reply. I dashed into the bathroom, grabbed him by the shoulders and dragged him to the divan. Then I ran to the telephone."

At the British Hospital in Cairo, where Emery was taken, the doctors diagnosed total paralysis of the right side and loss of speech. The following day, Thursday, March 11, 1971, W.B. Emery died.

"This strange event leads us to believe that the legendary curse of the Pharaohs has struck once again..." wrote the daily *Al Ahram* on March 12.

The latest victim of the curse was Kamal Mahrez. His death was reported in the *Parisien Libéré* of February 7, 1972: "We have heard from Cairo that Kamal Mahrez, Head of the Egyptian Antiquities Service, has recently died of a brain hemorrhage at the age of 52. His death revives speculation about the legend of Tutankhamen, Pharaoh of the 18th Dynasty, whose mummy has caused the death of almost all those connected with its discovery ... It is significant that Mr. Kamal Mahrez had recently signed with the British Museum an agreement to mount an exhibition of fifty objects from the tomb of Tutankhamen. He was the successor of Mr. Mohammed Mehdi, who also died of a brain hemorrhage just after approving a similar exhibition in Paris."

Chapter III

SCIENCE AND THE CURSE
OF THE PHARAOHS

F OR most archeologists, however, the so-called curse or
vengeance of the Pharaohs is pure speculation.

Some have tried to explain these strange deaths by scientific theories which, while they may not convince us, are certainly
interesting. The experts tend to see the curse as a generic term
covering strange or unknown phenomena, which it is nevertheless
possible to analyze scientifically.

Bats and the Curse

In 1956, Dr. Dean, senior doctor in the hospital of Port Elizabeth,
South Africa, put forward his theory of a virus found in the drop-
pings of bats and other rotting matter within the tombs.

To back up his theory, Dean claimed that the sickness caused by this virus—called histoplasmosis—produced symptoms like those observed among the victims of the curse: a raging fever and extreme exhaustion.

If, however, we wish to retain the idea of a curse uttered thousands of years ago, we must reject Dr. Dean's theory which treats it purely as a natural phenomenon.

Age-old poisons

More plausible is the poison theory. Almost certainly the Egyptians had knowledge of a certain number of poisons.

The fourth *Book of Moses* relates one of their customs, which was to force women found guilty of adultery to drink a poisonous liquid. Those who survived were declared innocent. The others, punished by the gods, died because they were guilty.

If there are few other examples of the Egyptians' knowledge and use of poisons it is because such a science would have been the exclusive domain of priests and sorcerers.

According to some experts, there is no reason why they could not have developed a detailed knowledge of poisons. The poisonous onion (Haemanthus toxicarius), the juice of which paralyzes the spine and affects the brain, was almost certainly known to the Egyptians, as were fruits like the corallodendron which contains a poison similar to curare. They also knew about the venom of the scorpion and a large number of snakes, spiders and toads which also caused paralysis of the nervous system.

Had some of these poisons been placed in the tombs? Would

they have remained powerful enough to cause death after thousands of years?

Absorption of these poisons through the mouth seems unlikely in the case of the archeologists. It would mean that certain objects had touched their lips, which seems unlikely.

But it is not necessary to swallow these poisons to be affected by them. They can be absorbed by perspiration or through small cuts on any part of the body.

If we suppose that certain walls or objects were covered in poison, it would be logical to explain the curse in this way.

The archeologists would certainly have perspired in the high temperatures of Egypt, and would probably have grazed their skin while moving objects in the tombs.

Recent research has shown that poisons, even when dried out, retain their potency for a long time.

Toxic gases and drugs

Other scientists have concentrated on the problem of poisonous gases.

This technique, according to some historians, was in use as early as the Middle Ages. The wick of a wax candle was dipped in arsenic and the vapor produced caused death.

Can we not suppose that similar candles might have been burned before the tombs were walled up?

It is also possible that capsules containing certain drugs obtained from wheat were scattered by the Ancients inside the tombs.

As these capsules decomposed, they would have released a nerve gas which causes a condition called ergot, involving gradual paralysis and eventual madness.

Why were the tombs sealed?

We might also suppose that the Egyptians used their knowledge of the harmful effects of mercury to protect the tombs.

Certain documents dating back to the 15th century B.C. reveal that the Egyptians had discovered mercury. Completely odorless, mercury, when it evaporates, destroys the cells of the nervous system and causes grave mental disorders.

Prussic acid, although not odorless, is just as dangerous as mercury. The Egyptians, claims the English chemist Humphrey, obtained it from the kernels of bitter almonds. It causes death by asphyxia. Some experts believe that the bandages in which the mummies were wrapped were impregnated with prussic acid.

In connection with these toxic gases, it is important to note that the tombs of the Pharaohs were hermetically sealed. This was, however, contrary to the teachings of Egyptian religion. The *Ka* must be able to come and go at will. Humphrey maintains that the Ancient Egyptians sealed the tombs in this way not to protect them from robbers, as is generally believed, but to maintain the potency of these gases.

A pyramid-shaped razor blade sharpener

In 1959, the Czech engineer Karel Drbal obtained a patent, number 91304, for a razor blade sharpener in the shape of a pyramid.

Like many other scientists throughout the world, Drbal was trying to prove that certain geometric shapes—in particular the pyramid—accumulate energy and act as a sort of condenser or lense.

Before him, the research of the Frenchman Jean Martial had proved that the period of mummification of bodies was considerably reduced inside pyramids.

Drbal pursued the experiments of Martial and constructed a cardboard pyramid 6 inches high and 10 inches from apex to base. He placed inside it a razor blade on a base 2 inches high. Within six days the blade was sharp. Both objects were placed on a north–south axis, like the pyramids of the Valley of the Kings.

This example of experimental physics led many to conclude that the Ancient Egyptians were well aware of such phenomena. Such phenomena can scarcely explain the Curse of the Pharaos, but do tell us something about the scientific achievements of Ancient Egypt.

A night in the Great Pyramid

The English researcher Paul Brunton, who also studied the strange phenomena connected with the pyramids, attempted an original experiment.

After several attempts, he obtained permission to spend a night in the royal chamber situated in the middle of the Pyramid of Cheops.

This is how Paul Brunton describes in his book *Search in Secret Egypt* the nightmares which he experienced during that memorable night. "Ghostly figures were everywhere in the darkness of the chamber; they swirled around me; the vague feeling of unease which I had experienced earlier proved to be entirely justified. The incredible tension made my heart beat like a hammer within my inert body. Fear of the supernatural, which affects us all, gripped me once more. Fear, fright, and terror persistently showed me their terrible faces. Without my wanting them to, my hands were clamped together like a vice. But I was determined to carry on; although these ghostly forms had terrified me at first, they eventually forced me to summon up all my reserves of courage and determination.

"My eyes were closed but these grey, gliding, fog-shrouded shapes pushed themselves into the field of my vision. And always there was this unrelenting hostility, this terrifying pressure to prevent me from carrying out my resolution.

"A circle of hostile creatures surrounded me, huge elemental creations, frightening figures of terror from the underworld, grotesque shapes, madmen, hulking and devilish apparitions passed around me, my whole being revolted. In a few moments I lived through an experience I shall never forget. This incredible scene remains imprinted on my memory. Nothing in the world could tempt me to repeat the experiment; I will never again spend a night in the Great Pyramid."

A deadly concentration of energy

Brunton's experiences were terrifying, even for a trained scientist. The terror which overwhelmed him caused these nightmarish visions.

But many other people have experienced some sort of disturbance inside the Great Pyramid.

H.V. Morton, in his book *Through the Lands of the Bible*, tells of his own experience.

While he was visiting the Pyramid of Cheops with a group of tourists, Morton was suddenly gripped by a sensation of panic and extreme exhaustion. He had to crawl out "on all fours," in his own words.

In the light of all this evidence, many experts have wondered whether the ancient Egyptians had accumulated certain forms of energy inside the tombs, energy capable of producing terrifying visions, and possibly the death of the intruders.

But here we are leaving the realm of scientific explanations and entering that of speculation and theory, where proof becomes impossible and faith takes over.

PART FOUR

CHAMPOLLION AND THE SECRET OF HIEROGLYPHICS

*"My knowledge of hieroglyphics is only
sufficiently advanced to realize the immense
progress I will need to make in order
to pick my way through the great labyrinth
of sacred writing. I can see the way ahead,
but I do not know whether the energies
of one man and his whole lieftime will be sufficient
for such a vast undertaking."*

Jean-François Champollion

Chapter I

THE FIRST ATTEMPTS
AT INTERPRETATION

WRITING probably first appeared in Egypt around the year 3200 B.C. It seems that after that far-off time, the Egyptians made rapid progress in this area. It had a religious significance for them. Knowledge of reading and writing was a means of understanding truth and the mysteries of religion.

Writing also had an administrative function, and appeared at the moment of the country's unification. This was no accident. Egyptian civilisation depended closely on the Nile and the best possible use of the river's waters. Dykes and dams had to be built to control its flow. The earth had to be leveled to spread the water evenly, and canals dug to carry it as far as possible.

All these operations required an efficient central administration, which in turn needed a simple medium of communication: in other words, writing.

More than 6,000 hieroglyphic signs

The Egyptians of the time of the Pharaohs carved their signs on wood or stone, or wrote on canvas or papyrus. A reed pen dipped into a wooden palette containing the colors was their main instrument, together with the stylus.

At first the priests were responsible for writing. Then, gradually, professional scribes took over.

The profession of scribe had great status and many privileges, among them exemption from paying taxes.

In rich families, only the sons learned to read and write in schools run by priests. It was a difficult subject: they had to learn 500 different signs.

And these were merely the starting point. In modern times, the French Institute of Oriental Archeology has recorded more than 6,000 hieroglyphics.

The sacred books of the Temple of Edfu

The science of writing, essentially religious in character, was developed inside buildings called "Houses of Life." There the sacred texts were studied, collected and transcribed. Inscriptions destined for monuments were also drafted there.

All the texts were classified, cataloged and stored in the rooms called "Houses of Books," which adjoined the temples.

Here is an extract from the list of sacred books in the Temple of Edfu, carved on the walls of the library:

This wooden, bituminized statuette was inlaid with gold. It was discovered in Tutankhamen's tomb. It represents the Pharaoh in the shape of the god Ihy, son of Hator, progressing towards his rebirth. To be reborn in Osiris, he has to pass again through the entire growth cycle. *The Cairo Museum, Ferni.*

"The papyrus and the great parchments
of pure hide, telling how to slay the evil spirit;
repel the crocodile;
conserve time;
preserve the boat;
the book of the King's procession;
the book of religious ceremonies;
how to protect the town, the house,
the white crown of the throne, the year;
the book containing all the secrets of science;
the secrets of divine offerings
in all their details;
the inventory of the temple;
the book of command over men;
the book of combat; how to decorate a wall;
how to protect the body;
a guide to the movements of the stars;
a list of all places,
and what is to be found there..."

The three types
of script

Thanks to the erudition of Clement of Alexandria—a father of the Church in the third century A.D.—we know of three types of Egyptian writing.

Hieroglyphics, in which each sign is drawn or engraved in great detail. This is the type of script found on temples, obelisks, statues and *stelae*.

Hieratic script, which was more like modern handwriting. It was written from right to left, in columns in ancient times, then, later, in lines.

Then, lastly, there was demotic, or popular script, which was even more like modern handwriting, and written from right to left in lines.

All three scripts were not in use at the same time, although hieroglyphics were used throughout Egyptian history. The forms of the hieroglyphs changed little during this long period, however, and they tended to become far too numerous in the hellenistic period which came towards the end of the Egyptian empire. Hieratic script appeared at about the same time as hieroglyphics. It was used above all for administrative and legal documents, but was also used in private correspondence, literature, religious and scientific treatises, works on medicine and magic, for example. It was the script used by the scribes of the "Houses of Life" in the temples. It was usually traced on papyrus or etched on fragments of earthenware or limestone *(ostraca)*. Sometimes it was carved on stone, notably in the outlying deserts.

Around the fourth century B.C. hieratic script began to degenerate. More and more cursive it became "abnormal hieratic" and then, from the third century B.C. onwards, demotic script. This replaced hieratic script in all legal, literary, scientific or privat documents.

The lost secret of hieroglyphics

Hieratic script was now used only for religious texts written on papyrus, hence the name "hieratic" (sacred writing) given to it by Clement of Alexandria.

The closing of the temples in the fourth century A.D. was the end of Egyptian writing.

The "Houses of Life," where scribes continued to copy hieratic texts and compose hieroglyphic inscriptions, were abolished and their inmates dispersed.

From the third century B.C., the Egyptians themselves had abandoned traditional forms of writing in favor of Greek characters, to which they added one or two signs from demotic script to convey sounds which were not present in Greek.

From this time on, the key to hieroglyphics was lost, and it would be necessary to wait almost 1,000 years before the inscriptions and texts from the time of the Pharaohs were understood once more.

Some incredible translations

We will quote just a few of the early attempts to decipher such texts.

In the seventeenth century, the German Jesuit Athanase Kircher, inventor of the magic lantern, professor at Würzburg and member of the *Collegium Romanum*, published in Rome four volumes of hieroglyphic translations, which later turned out to be inaccurate in every way. There are some gems in the "translations" of this worthy Jesuit.

A text which can be correctly rendered as: "everlasting are the aspects of the god Re, the beloved of Re," was interpreted by Kircher thus: "The celestial citadel of the planets is protected from all misfortunes by the intervention of the divine Osiris..."

He did, however, reach some correct conclusions: the derivation of Coptic from hieroglyphics, for example. We will say more of this later.

In the following century another "translator," this time an anonymous Frenchman, claimed to have found, among the hieroglyphics of the Temple of Dendera, the 100th Psalm.

At the same time, in Geneva, another publication appeared which was just as imaginative. The author claimed that the obelisk of Pamphylos was "an account, written 4,000 years before Christ, of the triumph of good over evil."

Finally, Abbe Tandeau de Saint-Nicolas claimed that hieroglyphics were not a form of writing at all, merely decoration!

Towards the end of the eighteenth century, the conclusions of other scholars can be taken more seriously. The Swede Akerblad, who had copied several hieroglyphics in Cairo, thought that they were a sort of alphabet and tried to figure it out, with some success.

The Dane Zoega claimed that certain signs represented the names of Kings, a theory which was supported by the French orientalists of the time, Abbé Barthélemy and Joseph de Guignes.

These two conclusions, more logical than those reached earlier, were still based more on intuition than on any systematic analysis.

But, despite all such attempts to decipher them, hieroglyphics continued to remain a mystery.

167 "Civilian Experts" recruited by Napoleon

We have to wait until Napoleon's campaign in Egypt and the discovery of the Rosetta Stone for the secret of hieroglyphics to be finally discovered.

On May 19, 1798, Napoleon left Toulon and set sail for Alexandria.

There were 328 vessels in his fleet, carrying no less than 38,000 men, including 167 "civilian experts" —called "donkeys" by the crew. There was also a library containing almost every work on Egypt published in France and Europe.

Among these experts, recruited for Napoleon by the efficient Monge, were the astonomers Quesnot and Mechin; the mathematicians Fourier, Costaz, Malus, de Villiers du Terrage, du Bois-Aymé and Viard; the chemists Berthollet, Champy, Regnault and Descotils; the engineers Conte and Cotelle; the architects Balzac and Lepère; the geographer Lecesne; the zoologist Geoffroy Saint-Hilaire; the botanist Coquebert de Mombret; the doctors Desgenettes and Larrey; the mineralogist Dolomieu; the artists Vivant-Denon, Joly, Dutertre and Redouté; the poet Perceval de Grandmaison; the orientalists Belletête, Delaporte, Jaubert and Venture; the musicians Rigel and Villoteau.

Napoleon, fascinated by the Orient, and versed in ancient history like all his contemporaries, was trying to emulate the great conquerers of the past. He would not be content to strike a blow against England by cutting off the route to the east, he would revive, at the same time, the splendors of Ancient Egypt. The team of experts had been recruited to assist him in this enterprise. They were to greatly enlarge our knowledge of the country, both past and present.

Between battles, Egypt is studied in great detail

At dawn on July 1, 1798, the fleet reached Alexandria. Soldiers, sailors, scholars and artists discovered the delights of this exotic land.

On July 21, around two in the afternoon, the army stood before Cairo, defended by the mamelukes, whose commander was the governor of Egypt, Murad Bey. After several attacks, the troops of Napoleon, spurred on by his famous phrase: "From the tops of these pyramids, fourteen centuries look down on you," entered the city in triumph. This was on July 25, and by now the control of the route to the East seemed assured.

But on August 1, the battle of Abukir marked the end of French illusions in Egypt. The British fleet under Nelson roundly defeated the squadron of Admiral Brueys.

The French army was marooned in Egypt, unable to leave and cut off from help. The French scholars made the most of this situation to compile a mass of documents, directed from Cairo by the Egyptian Institute, founded in 1798 by Napoleon.

The researchers set off to every part of the country. Between battles they sketched monuments, made surveys, took notes, interviewed the inhabitants. From June 1898 to September 1802, every aspect of Egypt was studied in detail.

"Hieroglyphics are an Insoluble Problem" (de Sacy)

Some years later, from 1809 to 1828, this knowledge was collected in a work entitled *Description de l'Egypte* comprising ten huge volumes of text and ten of illustrations[1].

The work weighed some 275 pounds, and the importance given to the maps and pictures required the creation of a new size of paper, the so-called "grand-Egypte."

Berthollet was the first editor of this enormous work; he was followed by Conte, then Lancret and François Jomard.

The *Description de l'Egypte* had a considerable effect in Europe. The West discovered an almost totally unknown world, which would remain unknown as long as the mystery of hieroglyphics remained unsolved.

The famous Parisian orientalist Silvestre de Sacy declared: "The problem is too complex and impossible to solve scientifically." One apparently insignificant incident was to prove de Sacy wrong.

---

1. These drawings were mostly the work of Dominique Vivant-Denon, of whom it was said that "he charged at the monuments like a soldier going into battle." His drawings of Egyptian monuments were a mine of information for scholars. Under the Monarchy, Vivant-Denon had earned a somewhat immoral reputation for his erotic novels, sold "under the counter." He later became curator of the Louvre Museum, which he enriched with works of art acquired during Napoleon's many campaigns.

A historic find

When the French fleet was defeated off Abukir, Napoleon, afraid that English troops might land, dug trenches in the Nile delta and had the forts strengthened to provide a better defense.

During the reconstruction of one of these forts, at the beginning of July 1799, a soldier stationed at the Fort de Saint-Julien, five miles to the northwest of a town called Rosetta, struck an object with the blade of his pickaxe.

He was surprised to see that the stone he had unearthed bore inscriptions like those he had already seen on certain monuments. He summoned an officer, Captain Bouchard, who decided to put the *stele* in a safe place.

Of black basalt and less than 12 inches thick, this stone soon became known as the Rosetta Stone. It bore three inscriptions, one above the other, in three different scripts. At the top were 14 lines of hieroglyphics; in the center, 32 lines of demotic script; and, at the bottom, a Greek text 54 lines in length.

The Greek, which was perfectly legible, could be used to translate the two other passages, since it seemed probable from the way in which they were arranged that the content of each passage was the same.

The providential decree of Ptolemy V

The Greek text was translated immediately. It concerned a decree of King Ptolemy V, issued at Memphis in 196 B.C.

It expressed the thanks of the priests of Memphis to the king, who, upon his recent accession to the throne, had granted the priests a series of favors, for example an amnesty on unpaid taxes, the distribution of large sums of money and the protection of their temples in time of war. In fact, Ptolemy had given the god Apis, or his priests, a gift far more valuable than any previously granted by an Egyptian king.

After passing through various hands, the Rosetta Stone reached Alexandria. General Menou, shortly to take over command of the French expedition upon Napoleon's return to France and Kleber's assassination, stressed the importance of the discovery. The stone was stored in a safe place. But it was not to remain for long in French hands.

An artillery detachment and a gun-carriage recover the Rosetta Stone

The French expedition was a failure. The English defeated Menou at Canopus in March 1801. The French Army surrendered at Cairo on June 27. In accordance with article 16 of the Act of Surrender, the victors confiscated all the antiquities collected by the French on Egyptian soil.

"The members of the Institute may take with them all the instruments which they brought from France, but the Arab manuscripts, statues and other collections made for the French Republic will be deemed public property, and will be at the disposal of the generals of the combined armies."

Sir Tomkyns Hilgrove Turner, charged with the mission of recovering these priceless archeological treasures, claimed the Rosetta Stone from the French.

General Menou, arguing that the stone was his personal property, refused to hand it over to the English. "When the French realized that we were going to confiscate the treasures," wrote Turner[1], "the packing which protected the stone was removed and the stone itself was overturned. The packing cases containing the other objects were smashed. From the start, infinite pains had been taken to protect the antiquities from any damage. I protested on several occasions, but the main cause of difficulty was the stone . . .

"When I told Lord Hutchinson of the manner in which the stone had been treated, he gave me a detachment of artillery and a gun-carriage to go to General Menou's residence. I took possession of the stone that evening with no mishap, but with several problems of transport through the narrow streets, amid the jeers of French officers and men."

The Rosetta Stone
given to George III

Before the stone was put on board ship for England, a delegation of French scholars, led by Marcel and Galland, came to see

---

1.   An account of the transactions concerning the Rosetta Stone, compiled by H. Turner and addressed to the secretary of the Society of Antiquaries, of London, on May 30, 1810.

Turner and asked to make impressions of the stone so that they too could study it.

Turner accepted, on condition that the stone should not suffer from the operation. Marcel, in charge of printing for the expedition, decided to use the face of the stone as a "plate" and to cover it in ink. This would provide a large number of copies in a short space of time.

And so several copies of the Rosetta Stone reached Paris while the original was sent to London under the supervision of Lord Hutchinson himself. It was presented to George III, who donated it to the British Museum.

In every country men studied the drawings, copies and imprints of the stone in an attempt to unravel its secret.

Some of these interpretations are highly original. For example Count Paulin claimed to have deciphered in a single night the hieroglyphics on the stone, thanks to Horapollon[1], Pythagoras and the Kabbala!

Other studies were more interesting. The Swedish diplomat and philologist Akerblad, starting from the demotic script of the stone and comparing it with the Greek text, succeeded in identifying the words "temple" and "Greek."

The Englishman Thomas Young, physicist, doctor and philologist, identified the hieroglyph of King Ptolemy, and, from this starting-point, drew up a list of 221 symbols of which 77 were later found to be correct.

---

1.   In the 4th century B.C., the Greek compiler Horapollon attempted in vain to decipher the hieroglyphics.

But these isolated results did not permit the claim that the problem of translating hieroglyphics had been solved.

CHAPTER II

CHAMPOLLION – ANOTHER VICTIM OF THE CURSE OF THE PHARAOHS?

THE man destined to penetrate the mysteries of hieroglyphics was a mere youth when the *Courrier de l'Egypte* published, on "the 29th day of Fructidor, in the 7th year of the Republic," an article on the discovery of the Rosetta Stone some 27 days earlier. But, already, he showed signs of great intellectual ability.

This young genius, whose name is forever linked with the science of Egyptology, was called Jean-François Champollion. The circumstances of his birth were rather exceptional.

The strange prediction of Jacquou the sorcerer

In the middle of 1790, the wife of the bookseller Jacques Champollion was in great pain. Her half-paralyzed body no longer obeyed her, and she had to remain in bed. Her husband called the doctor, but with no result. He decided, as was usual in the region, to call in the sorcerer.

The next day Jacquou the healer was at the poor woman's bedside. He examined her and asked her questions, then he scattered medicinal herbs on the bed.

"Lie on these herbs and drink this glass of mulled wine," he ordered the patient. "In three days your sickness will be cured... I also predict the birth of a son. His renown will be great and he will be the light of centuries to come."

And indeed three days later the sick woman was on her feet and, some months later, on December 23, 1790, at two in the morning, a son was born who was christened Jean-François.

The doctor who attended the confinement noticed that the baby had a yellow cornea, and that his dark complexion and his features were strangely Oriental[1].

At the age of five, Jean-François could read

From his early years, Jean-François astounded those around him.

At the age of five he was able to read whole passages from the Bible, although he had never been taught to read. On his own, abandoning his toys, he had taught himself to read by comparing the written text with the passages from the Bible which his mother read to him each evening, and which he learned by heart.

---

1.   Some years later, because of these features, his friends and relations were to nickname him "the Egyptian."

He was seven years old when he heard the word Egypt for the first time. His brother, Jacques-Joseph[1], 12 years his senior, was fascinated by the country. He had studied Egyptian Art and dreamed of joining the expedition organized by Napoleon; but he was turned down, and settled in Grenoble to devote himself to the study of archeology.

He did not hesitate to sacrifice his own career for that of Jean-François, whose genius he was among the first to recognize.

In 1801, the child—now in his eleventh year—set off to join his brother in Grenoble. Jacques-Joseph thought that the climate would suit his brother, whose progress in school had been disappointing.

Jean-François, confronted with hieroglyphics for the first time, says: "I shall read them!"

There was one subject, however, in which Jean-François excelled: languages.

He had already mastered in spectacular fashion Greek and Latin. When he arrived in Grenoble, he began to study Hebrew.

During a school inspection, Fourier, who, as we have seen, had been part of the expedition to Egypt, questioned Jean-François. The boy, carried along by his brother's enthusiasm, had been fascinated for some time by everything relating to Egypt.

---

1. Later on, to distinguish him from his younger brother, Jacques-Joseph had himself called Champollion-Figeac.

Jean-François was a thin, almost sickly youth, but he was far from timid.

Fourier was amazed at the maturity and knowledge of this schoolboy. He invited him to his house and showed him, to his great astonishment, the treasures which he had brought back from Egypt.

"Can you read that?" looking at a papyrus covered in hieroglyphics.

"No," replied Fourier, "not yet. I fear it will be many years before that is possible."

With both fists clenched and a frown on his face, Jean-François declared, "I shall read it in a few years from now, when I am fully grown."

At 17, Champollion speaks twelve languages

In addition to his passion for Egypt, the young Champollion demonstrated his insatiable curiosity in a number of subjects.

At the age of 12, for example, he wrote his first book, *The History of Famous Dogs*. At 13, he learned new languages: Arabic, Syrian, Chaldean and, above all, Coptic, the language of Egyptian Christians. He was convinced that the Jesuit Kircher was right to see in it the final form of the language of Ancient Egypt.

With the assistance of Fourier, he managed to consult various texts and compiled, after much study, the first map of the Empire of the Pharaohs.

His linguistic knowledge continued to expand: at the age of 17

The *Ka*, Tutankhamen's eternal double. The fate of those who had discovered his tomb, most of whom died a sudden and mysterious death, lends some credence to the hypothesis of the "curse of the Pharaohs."
The Cairo Museum, Ferni.

he could speak twelve languages, most of them fluently. The most familiar of these was without doubt Coptic. He wrote: "I amuse myself by translating everything that comes into my head into Coptic. I speak Coptic to myself, since nobody else would understand me."

A member of the Academy of Grenoble at the age of 17

Jean-François felt that he would have to go to Paris. There he would be able to consult the documents which were not available in Grenoble.

But the Academy of Grenoble wanted a thesis from him. Jean-François presented the introduction to the book he was busy writing, *Egypt under the Pharaohs*[1]. The thesis was well argued and illustrated.

The young man was unanimously elected a member of the Academy. Renaudon, the President, embraced him, declaring: "If the Academy receives you as a member despite your extreme youth, it is in consideration of what you have done. But we are counting more on what you are capable of achieving. We are convinced that

---

1.   The book was finished by the end of 1808 and published 6 years later, in 1814. It established the geography of Egypt on the basis of Coptic documents. Thirty copies of its Introduction were printed separately, beginning 1811. It contained a synonymical table of Coptic, Greek and local names of the towns of Egypt.

you will justify our faith in you, and that you will remember, when your work has made your reputation, that it was the Academy of Grenoble which gave you your first chance.''

Intensive study

A few days later, Jean-François set off for Paris, accompanied by his brother.

During the journey, which lasted seventy hours, Jacques-Joseph explained to his brother the life he would lead in Paris. ''You will be joining the Collège de France. Tomorrow I will introduce you to your professor, M. de Sacy... I have found you a room near the Louvre. The landlady, Madame Mecran, is a good woman and has been recommended to me. The small rent she is asking will allow you to spend more money on the books you will need.''

Jean-François was already dreaming of these books, and the wonderful libraries he would be able to use in the capital. When his brother returned to Grenoble, Jean-François began a period of intensive study. He hurried from one library to another. Just as in his childhood he forgot all distractions, preferring instead the dusty atmosphere of the archives to any social life.

To amuse himself, he borrowed a Chinese grammar from his brother. He ran out of money. Jacques-Joseph helped him as best he could, but it was not enough. During the winter of 1807 he fell seriously ill and was considerably weakened as a result.

Alexandre Lenoir,
the impostor

At the start of 1808, Napoleon, who was about to set off for Spain, called to the flag all males over the age of 16. Jean-François was furious.

"I have lost so much time already because of my illness. I cannot abandon my research yet again!"

He wrote several desperate letters to his brother. Jacques-Joseph stepped in, writing letter after letter to his friends and relations, compiling petitions. He finally reached his objective. Jean-François was exempted from military service.

His research soon led him to a conclusion about the nature of hieroglyphics: the script did not consist merely of symbols. By comparing a recent copy of the Rosetta Stone with a papyrus in Coptic, he discovered eight personal pronouns corresponding to phonetic signs. Jean-François was jubilant. His research was beginning to bear fruit. Unable to contain himself, he went out for a walk, enjoying for the first time in many weeks the Paris which surrounded him. During his walk he met one of his friends, who seemed excited by something. "Have you heard the news?" asked his friend. "Alexandre Lenoir has found the secret of hieroglyphics!" Jean-François was dumbfounded. "No, its not possible!"

"Yes, he has. His work was published in the *Nouvelle Explication* this morning."

Jean-François dashed to buy a copy of the journal. Back in his room, he scanned the pages eagerly.

Suddenly, he began to laugh. Alexandre Lenoir was an impostor, and his "complete interpretation" of hieroglyphics a hoax. Jean-François could pursue his own research. The mystery was still unresolved.

Politician, scholar and man of letters

On July 10, 1809, Champollion returned to Grenoble, where he had been appointed Professor of History at the University. He was then only 19. His pupils were at least 17, and inevitably his colleagues were jealous, all the more because the revolutionary theories which he put forward during his classes troubled them. In addition to this, it was common knowledge in Grenoble that he hated Napoleon (he had written certain satires directed against him), and that he hated the Bourbons equally.

By means of intrigue involving politics, self-interest and gossip, his enemies had his salary reduced. To make ends meet Champollion wrote plays, composed sonnets, music and revolutionary songs, which he did his best to sell.

Exiled for treason

On March 7, 1815, Napoleon stopped at Grenoble on his way to Paris. He was looking for a secretary. Thanks to the Mayor of Grenoble the post was given to Jacques-Joseph, who was, for his part, still a fervent admirer of Napoleon.

Champollion was present at the interview between Napoleon and his brother. The Emperor, who wanted to know more about this scholar who had the reputation of being obsessed by egyptology, questioned him closely and learned that he was working on a Coptic dictionary. He promised to have it published[1].

But the "Hundred Days" were soon over. The Bourbons returned to Paris. Napoleon was exiled to Saint Helena and Jacques-Joseph was prosecuted for having acted as his secretary.

Jean-François was scarcely in a better position. True to his convictions, he had urged the population of Grenoble to offer resistance during the siege of the town by the Royalists. This action led to his exile for high treason. It lasted for eighteen months. When he returned to France in 1818, he lived alternately in Paris and Grenoble, fleeing the creditors who hounded him.

Despite all these difficulties, the young scholar continued his work on Ancient Egypt.

The name of Cleopatra

He was the first to prove, in two papers which he addressed to the "Académie royale d'Inscriptions et Belles-Lettres," that hieratic and demotic script were not alphabetical but ideographic.

Spurred on by this success, he turned to the intensive study of

---

1.   This planned publication of a Coptic dictionary never materialized because of the jealousy of Champollion's colleagues. He wrote: "There goes my project, cast before the voracious jaws of the wolves and exposed to the malicious scribbling of my vulgar critics."

hieroglyphics. He learned them by heart, and tried to penetrate their structure.

At the end of the summer of 1822, he decided to compare the hieroglyph of King Ptolemy discovered by Thomas Young with the hieroglyphics found on an obelisk unearthed at Philae, an island near the first cataract on the Nile, by the architect Banks. On this obelisk, which was exhibited in London, was the name of Ptolemy followed by another "cartouche," or frame, which he imagined to contain the name of Cleopatra. "The hieroglyphic text of the Rosetta Stone," Champollion explained later, "which would have been ideal for this piece of research, only contained the name of Ptolemy, because of the cracks on its surface.

"The obelisk of Philae also contains the name of Ptolemy, with the same hieroglyphic form as on the Rosetta Stone, also framed by a cartouche, and it is followed by a second cartouche which probably contains the name of a woman, a queen, since it ends with the hieroglyphic signs for the feminine gender, signs which are found in the names of all Egyptian goddesses. The obelisk was fixed to a base, or so it is said, bearing a Greek inscription which was a petition from the priests of Isis at Philae, addressed to King Ptolemy, Cleopatra, his sister and Cleopatra his wife. If this obelisk and the hieroglyphic inscription which it bore were a result of the petition of the priests, who spoke of the consecration of such a monument, the cartouche containing the feminine proper noun could only be the symbol for Cleopatra."

Champollion identifies 12 letters

In Greek, the names of Cleopatra and Ptolemy have several identical letters. And if the signs which were similar in the two cartouches represented the same sounds, it would mean that they were entirely phonetic.

"A preliminary comparison," wrote Champollion, "revealed that, in demotic script, the two names written phonetically contained several identical characters. The analogies between the general structure of these three Egyptian scripts should indicate the same repetition in the hieroglyphic form of the names. This was immediately confirmed by comparing the cartouche containing the name of Ptolemy with the cartouche on the obelisk of Philae which we supposed, according to the Greek inscription, to contain the name of Cleopatra."

Thanks to this comparison, the hieroglyphics *Ptolemaios* and *Kleopatra* were revealed and Champollion had discovered 12 letters: p, t, l, m, i, s, k, e, a, r, o and another t.

"I've got it!" exclaimed Champollion

Despite this remarkable breakthrough Champollion was not at the end of his labors. Many signs still remained to be deciphered.

He continued his research. On September 14, 1822, his friend, the architect Jean-Nicolas Huyot, gave him two copies of cartouches containing the names of Pharaohs, discovered in Lower Nubia.

On the first of these was an ibis, a creature representing the god Thot, and on the second was a sun. Champollion immediately deciphered these as the names of two famous Pharaohs: Thutmose and Rameses. He also noticed that another element was common to both inscriptions. Champollion took this to correspond to the sound *mes*.

Suddenly, it became clear.

"I've got it!" he exclaimed. "There are phonetic signs, but also ideograms and signs combining two consonants."

Dropping paper and pencil, he rushed to tell the news to his brother in the Institute's library.

The emotion was too much for him. "At that moment," his brother wrote later, "a physical and mental collapse overtook the author of this great discovery. His legs gave way; his mind grew dull. He was put to bed—his first moment of repose after fifteen years of exhausting mental effort."

This seizure lasted for sixty hours, but on September 27, 1822, Champollion gave his publisher the text of his famous *Lettre à M. Dacier relative à l'alphabet des hiéroglyphes phonétiques*, which he had taken just three days to write. Then he went to the "Académie des Inscriptions," where, to the amazement of the academicians, he read this paper for the first time. It contained, in 52 pages, the complete hieroglyphic alphabet as well as an explanation of the Egyptian system of writing. The *Lettre* is now a revered document among Egyptologists.

Champollion defended by the Pope

Before the end of 1823, the *Précis du système hiérogly-phique*, developing the ideas of the *Lettre*, was finished. It did not appear, however, until mid-April 1824. Scholars could now judge this extraordinary discovery on its merits.

Some of them continued to think that Champollion had not com-pletely solved the problem. The "Hyksos" and the "Unclean," as the young scholar called them, were many in number.

There were sceptics, like Etienne Quatremère, who condemned the new explanation without examining it. There were hostile oppo-nents, like Klaproth the "Tartar," who only studied the discoveries of the "Egyptian" in order to challenge them. He did so with a venom which continued even after the death of Champollion. There were those who resented the fact that their own systems had been demolished by Champollion's explanation, such as Spohn, Seyffarth, Gulianov, Köller, Ungarelli and Lanci. There were also certain theolo-gians who feared that the chronology of the Bible might be challenged. These fears reached the ears of the Pope, who, against the wishes of the theologians, was not worried about the Bible and sprang to the defense of Champollion, "who has put an end to Zodiacomania[1]." There was also a large body of people unwilling to accept new ideas.

---

1. The deriders of the Bible, at the start of the 19th century, had based themselves on the Egyptian Zodiac of Dendera to criticize it. Cham-pollion had demonstrated that this Zodiac did not belong to Ancient Egypt but dated back, at the most, to the Roman occupation of the countries of the Nile. This sculpted Zodiac of Dendera had been moved to the Lou-vre in 1822.

Sylvestre de Sacy pays homage to Champollion

Thomas Young, for his part, felt cheated. Had he not successfully identified certain letters? Was he not the predecessor of Champollion in the science of hieroglyphics?

The enemies of the young scholar gave their support to Young. "Monsieur Champollion," wrote Gulianov, "wishes the whole world to think that he was the first to unravel the mysteries of hieroglyphics. And what of the work of Thomas Young? Should it not take precedence? Should we not give the English Egyptologist credit for this discovery?"

Luckily there were some who were not blinded by jealousy, among them the great Sylvestre de Sacy. In the *Journal des Savants* of March 1825, he wrote: "Champollion has, in my opinion, proved conclusively that, notwithstanding certain slight similarities between the results of Mr. Young's work and those which he has obtained from the discovery for which he should be given full credit, their methods are basically different. If Champollion had taken the ideas of Mr. Young as the basis of his own work, he would have proceeded in the wrong direction, and would merely have added to the mass of speculation which hieroglyphics have given rise to. We trust that this opinion will be confirmed by all scholars, of whatever nationality, who will consider objectively the respective rights of Mr. Young and M. Champollion to claim the right of having discovered the key to the ancient writings of Egypt."

A quarrel stirred up by the Press

Despite these repeated attacks by his enemy, Champollion had a high regard for Young. He even attempted a reconciliation.

"I am inclined," he wrote to a friend, "to give full credit to Dr. Young and have no desire to foment this literary quarrel, which would have been better confined to the two people concerned. It is the Press which has encouraged it. For my part, I no longer think about it, and am quite prepared to resume relations with Young—who was the first to break off contact—and to revive the friendly relationship which we had. Science would only gain from this reconciliation, and I have just taken the first step by writing to him to offer my services in Paris, and to obtain for him the moulds or drawings of monuments which may interest him. It is now up to him to restore the relationship, and you will see that I am not to blame if the affair does not turn out as I wish in all sincerity."

A wise reconciliation

A few days later, Champollion, in his *Discours d'ouverture du Cours d'Archéologie du Collège de France*, on May 10, 1831, paid tribute to Young, "whose useful research will assure for England an honorable place in Egyptology."

Then he proceeded to explain the theories of Young: "This scholar has brought to the study of the three texts on the Rosetta Stone a methodical approach embracing an extensive knowledge of physics and mathematics. He recognized, by a straightforward comparison, the groups of characters in the demotic inscription and the hiero-glyphic inscription corresponding to the words used in the Greek inscription. This work, the result of a highly intelligent comparison, suceeded in establishing certain notions about the characteristics of the different branches of Egyptian writing, and the connection between them. He provided material evidence confirming the idea of the Ancients about the use of figurative and symbolic characters in hieroglyphics. But the detailed structure of this form of writing, its con-nection with the spoken language, the number, the essence and the combination of its basic elements, remained vague and hypothetical."

"The road from Memphis to Thebes passes through Turin"

Scarcely had Champollion completed his *Précis du Système Hiérogly-phique*, that he was planning to pursue his work by com-piling a grammar.

The documents which he had were inadequate, however. Apart from the copies of the Rosetta Stone and the obelisk of Philae, the only material then available in France were a few copies of hiero-glyphic texts from the tomb of Seti I, the father of the great Rameses II.

For some time Champollion had thought of traveling to Italy in order to consult the documents he needed. Thanks to the generous friendship of the Duke of Blacas, a close companion of Louis XVIII and a great patron of archeology, he managed to travel to

Turin, where the magnificent collection of Egyptian antiquities made by Drovetti and acquired by the King of Sardinia-Piedmont was kept.

Once there, he was thrilled. "The road from Memphis to Thebes passes through Turin," he wrote. After making a detailed study of numerous texts, Champollion proved that Egyptian writing had evolved through the centuries, and the different scripts had developed special characteristics according to their use.

When he returned from Turin, he acquired for France the collection of Egyptian antiquities made by Salt, which he presented to the public in Paris in 1826, the year in which he was appointed Curator of Egyptology at the Louvre.

But his journey to Italy had made him eager to travel to Egypt. Would he ever set foot in this land so rich in written monuments?

"I can read hieroglyphics more fluently than I had dared to imagine"

His ambition was fulfilled in July 1828.

A Franco-Tuscan expedition, with fourteen members including Champollion, set off for Alexandria and arrived there on August 18.

This was Champollion's great moment. Not only because of the monuments he explored, but also because he confirmed his theories with each successive discovery. "I am so proud," he wrote to his brother, "having followed the Nile from its estuary to the second cataract, I can now tell you that there is nothing to modify in our *Letter*. Our alphabet is correct, and can be applied with equal success to the Egyptian monuments of Roman times and the inscriptions in every temple, palace and tomb from the days of the Pharaohs."

His hopes had been fulfilled beyond his wildest dreams. "Having spent six months among the monuments of Egypt," he exulted, "I am amazed by how much I can read, and far more fluently than I had dared to imagine."

The death of Champollion—the curse of the Pharaohs?

One thing worried him, however: he witnessed the destruction of fourteen temples by Moslem fanatics.

Champollion tried to convince Mohammed Ali, the ruler of Egypt, of the need to prevent such acts of vandalism. "It is high time to put an end to this barbarous destruction," he argued. "To achieve this end, His Highness should decree that no brick or stone should be removed on any pretext from existing ancient monuments."

When he left the country in December 1829, Mohammed Ali had as yet done nothing to remedy the situation. It would be another twenty years before the famous archeologist Mariette secured the preservation of ancient monuments.

Another setback came when the boat carrying the expedition reached Toulon. Passengers and crew had to stay on board in quarantine. The boat had no heating, although it was the middle of winter. The precarious health of Champollion was severely affected by the cold.

In 1831, he was appointed professor at the Collège de France, but was unable to teach classes and gave lectures instead.

On March 4, 1832, Champollion died at the age of 42. The cause of his illness was never established. Some have attributed it to the curse of the Pharaohs. "One cannot unveil with impunity the secrets of Egyptian writing," wrote the occultist Jacques Roubet. "Champollion paid with his life for his intrusion into the sacred mysteries of the Pharaohs.

"Was he cut off in his prime just as he was about to enter the 'forbidden area' of Egyptian occult science?

"Was he about to discover certain secrets which no man should ever know? The death of Champollion remains an enigma, and those who have studied his life have apparently neglected to examine the real cause of his death."

Théodule Déveria 1852

The French orientalist, Jean-François Champollion (1790-1832) was first to decipher the Egyptian hieroglyphics. He died at the age of 40; the cause of his disease could not be established with certainty. According to some, the scholar "paid with his life for his intrusion into the sacred mysteries of the Pharaohs." The portrait shown here is a drawing done by Théodule Devéria. *Roger-Viollet*.

PART FIVE

AT THE SOURCES
OF THE EGYPTIAN MYSTERIES

"By a close study of the monuments of the Ancient Empire, we are led to the inescapable conclusion that they do not represent the humble beginnings of Egyptian science and civilization, but rather the culmination of a highly developed culture, which, with consummate pride, wished to bequeath to other civilisations a supreme example of its superiority before it finally disappeared."

Matila Ghyka

Chapter I

THE LONG NIGHT
OF PREHISTORY

THE origins of Ancient Egypt are lost in the mist of time, and all the efforts of archeologists have failed to date precisely the birth and development of this strange civilization. There are two diametrically opposed schools of thought: the classical school and the so-called "hermetic" or "esoteric" school.

Menes, the first King of Egypt

The first school, which includes the majority of scholars and Egyptologists, places the beginnings of Egyptian civilization around 4,000 years before Christ.

In those far-off days, there were originally two kingdoms in the valley of the Nile. The Northern Kingdom had as its capital the present-day town of Tell Balamun, and its chief god was Horus. The Southern Kingdom worshipped the god Seth, and its capital was

Ombos, which corresponds to the present-day town of Kom Belal. A war eventually broke out between the two kingdoms. The North was victorious, replaced the cult of Seth by that of Horus and united the land under the same crown.

This unity was not to last for long. A second war ended with the victory of the Southerners, under King Narmer. They moved north and occupied the delta, an episode depicted on a votive palette in the temple of the goddess Nekhbet, near Edfu. But the first king to successfully unify the land and put an end to civil war was Menes, the first "historical" King of Egypt.

Recorded in Herodotus and Manetho, his name has also come down to us in certain papyri preserved in Turin. He was said to come from a town called This, the precise location of which is still unknown. After living in the South, Menes moved up to the delta, and built on the boundary of the two former kingdoms, at the apex of the delta, a new royal residence, the "White Wall," later to become Memphis.

Egyptian civilization takes shape

We know very little about the successors of Menes. Neither their names, nor the order in which they succeeded each other is known for sure. Archeologists have in fact adopted the dynastic tables established in the third century B.C. by Manetho, the Egyptian historian, who classified these kings into two dynasties.

Under these dynasties, Egyptian civilization gradually took shape: the appearance of writing, the construction of *mastabas*, the consolidation of royal power in the form of a strong central administration, the birth of fine arts and medicine, the organization of agriculture, thanks to the calendar which predicted the rise and fall of the Nile. In short, all the constituent parts of that civilization are present from this time. Then came the death of the last king of the second dynasty, who was replaced by the great King Djoser, the first, powerful Pharaoh of the third dynasty.

402,000 years before the Flood

All this is absurd, according to the supporters of the other theory, who believe, more or less, that the real history of Egypt goes far beyond the fourth millenium.

According to this school of thought, a highly developed civilization preceded the first two dynasties by tens of thousands of years. The traces of this civilization cannot be dated by carbon 14[1]. To understand it we must turn to occult doctrines, literature and legend.

What was Mme Blavatsky's interpretation, supported by the American "seer" Edgar Cayce?

The famous theosophist claimed that tens of thousands of years ago, the Lemurians——the third original race——abandoned their flooded country and crossed India to settle on the Nile. One of their kings reigned over Egypt 402,000 years before the Flood.

---

1. According to these esoterists, the dating by carbon 14 does not go back beyond 30,000 years B.C.

Edgar Cayce, the "sleeping prophet"

Without going back quite as far as Mme Blavatsky, Edgar Cayce also placed the origin of Egyptian civilization in the remote past.

Before his death in 1945, Cayce, dubbed "the sleeping prophet," "the greatest visionary in America," "the man of mystery" and even "the man who sees tomorrow, today and yesterday," devoted a number of "lectures" given under self-hypnosis to the origins of Egypt.

Egypt and North Africa, according to Cayce, were covered in water apart from the Sahara and certain areas of the Upper Nile Valley. After many centuries, and the emergence of new land in the area, the first King of Egypt appeared. His name was Raai, and he possessed great wisdom and spirituality, being "capable of understanding the universal laws."

From the start of his reign, he endeavored to teach his subjects about the "divine spark" which they carried within them. For this reason, he organized a meeting of "world leaders." Forty-four priests, prophets and astrologers met in Egypt to discuss ways and means of speeding up the development of mankind, to help him face up to physical conditions and to try to solve the problem of wild animals. The theme of the conference, chosen by Raai, dealt with the spiritual powers of man which make him the supreme being on Earth.

Thus began, for the first time on Earth, the study of the spiritual nature of man. "Raai," said Cayce, "defined relations between men and between man and the Infinite; the division of the mind into its conscious, sub-conscious and super-conscious parts; the different levels of learning and existence through which men had to pass in order to develop. These doctrines governed most phases of man's life on Earth, symbolized by the sun, moon, stars and elements. The inscription of the spiritual laws on stone or slate tablets was the first Bible. It was the first chapter of the *Book of the Dead*, as it was later to be called, but which had nothing funereal about it.

According to the "sleeping prophet" this conference took place in 37,842 B.C.!

The travel diary of Herodotus

The "prophecies" of Cayce and the ideas of Mme Blavatsky are confirmed to some extent by two ancient authors whose *bona fides* cannot be doubted. They are Herodotus, the "father of history," and the philosopher Plato.

Herodotus visited Egypt at the beginning of the 5th century B.C. His travels took him to the land of the Scythians, north of the Black Sea, then to Syria and Babylonia. He spent some time in Egypt, traveled along the Nile, as far as the first cataract—near the Isle of Elephantine. His main aim was to record for posterity the war between Greece and Persia, but, like a journalist, he provided fascinating and colorful reports of everything he saw and heard. Twenty-five centuries later, these accounts have lost none of their freshness, and archeological research has confirmed their basic accuracy.

This extraordinary travel diary was written with such flair and narrative skill that when Herodotus read it before an audience at

Olympia the young Thucydides was moved to tears and inspired to write his own History.

"The sun had departed from its course on four occasions"

This is what Herodotus wrote in the second book of his inquiry into the age of Egyptian civilization, which apparently fascinated him: "The Egyptians proved that there had been 341 generations of men between the first king and the last, the priest of Hephaistos. Three hundred generations correspond to ten thousand years, that is to say three generations every 100 years. Thus, for the 41 generations to be added to the 300, we must allow another 1,340 years. This gives a total of 11,340 years. The Egyptians declared that during that period no god had taken human form to rule the country. They also said that, during those 11,340 years, the sun had departed from its course on four occasions. It used to rise where it now sets, and set where it now rises. But this had caused no disturbance in Egypt, neither to rivers, nor to crops, nor where sickness and death were concerned."

The ancient archives of the Theban priests

The priests of Thebes, who gave this information to the Greek historian, also showed him 345 huge wooden statues representing the great priests, who were descended from father to son. "They were noble and good, but far from godlike. But before them," added the priests of Thebes, "there had been an era when the rulers of Egypt were gods, and these gods lived among men. The last of them to reign over Egypt was Horus, son of Osiris, whom the Greeks called Apollo."

And in order to prevent his readers from questioning these vast periods of time, Herodotus states that he has every confidence in the priests of Thebes. "Osiris corresponds to the Greek Dionysos. Dionysos, the youngest of the gods, was already 15,000 years old at the time of King Amasis. The Egyptians claim to know these things with certainty because they have counted these years and kept archives."

The journey of Solon to Egypt

The account of Herodotus resembles that given by Solon if we are to believe Plato.

This famous Athenian legislator (644 to 560 B.C.), Plato tells us in one of his dialogues, cannot be suspected of inventing a whole history. Solon traveled to Egypt around 590 B.C. At that time the Greeks were welcome in Egypt. The Pharaoh Amosis was known for his pro-Greek policies. He had granted important concessions to the free port of Naucratis, which, according to Herodotus, was the only stronghold of Greek trade in Egypt. Naucratis had been created many years before—probably in 630 B.C.—after the arrival of the Milesians in Egypt, and we have convincing archeological evidence to prove that Greeks from various regions were already living there when Solon arrived. Naucratis was a prosperous expanding city, on the west fork of the Nile about eleven miles from Saïs, and it is probable that the ship carrying Solon had come to unload its cargo there. From Naucratis, Solon, according to Plato, could easily travel to Saïs, at that time the administrative capital of Egypt.

Solon consults the priests of the goddess Neith

It was there that the Athenian legislator made contact with the Egyptian priests who took a keen interest in the history of their country. He was able to talk to them easily and at great length, thanks to the many interpreters trained in the special school founded by Psammetichus I to pursue the pro-Greek policies of the Saite kings.

That is why it is not impossible to imagine Solon consulting Egyptian historians and archivists, and even the priests of the goddess Neith, as Plato says. During these conversations, Solon took notes which he brought back to Alexandria with the intention of writing an epic poem on the theme of the conflicts of early history. Unfortunately his political commitments, or possibly his great age, prevented him from completing this project. He merely recounted to an ancestor of Plato what he had been told, and the account, possibly accompanied by a manuscript, was handed down until it was finally made public by Plato in one of his dialogues.

"You Greeks are still children"

Plato tells in the words of Critias the famous meeting between Solon and the Egyptian priests.

They explained to Solon how the Egyptian people had managed to survive all natural disasters. Thanks to the Nile, "the savior who protects the Egyptians from all catastrophes," these privileged witnesses of human history recorded in writing all the important events since the most distant times.

"There is in Egypt, in the delta, at the fork of the Nile, a region of which the main town is Saïs, birthplace of King Amosis. The inhabitants honor as the founder of their town a goddess whose Egyptian name is Neith, and who is known in Greek as Athena. They are fond of the Athenians and claim a kinship with them. His travels having taken him to this town, Solon related to me how he was received with great ceremony; then, having closely questioned the priests with a special knowledge of antiquity, he discovered that neither he nor any other Greek knew anything about them. Another day, wishing to encourage the priests to talk about ancient history, he started talking about our own knowledge of the distant past. He spoke of Phoroneus, who was supposed to have been the first man, and of Niobe, then he related how Deucalion and Pyrrha survived the Deluge; he traced the genealogy of their descendants and tried, by counting the generations, to work out how many years had elapsed since these events.

"Then one of the priests, who was very old, said to him: 'Ah, Solon! You Greeks are still children and there are no old men in Greece.' 'What do you mean?' asked Solon. 'You are young in spirit,' answered the priest. 'You have no time-honored opinions, and no science dimmed by time. And the reason is this: there have often been and will often be disaster affecting men, the greatest caused by fire and water, the rest by a thousand other things. For example, you have the story of Phaeton, son of the Sun, who one day harnessed his father's chariot, but, unable to keep it on course, set fire to everything on Earth and died himself, struck by a thunderbolt.

" 'This story seems a fable, but the truth which it contains is that the heavenly bodies which revolve around the Earth deviate from their course, and a great conflagration destroys from time to time what is on the surface of the Earth. Then those who live in the mountains and high, arid places perish rather than those living beside rivers and seas.

"Everything has been recorded in our temples since time immemorial"

" 'We Egyptians have the Nile, our savior, who protects us from such disasters by its flooding. When, on the other hand, the gods submerge the Earth, to purify it, the inhabitants of mountain regions escape death; but those who live in our towns are carried off by the waters of the river towards the sea. But, in our case, the water does not come down from the mountains, but, on the contrary, rises naturally from below. This is why the oldest traditions are preserved by us. But in every place where excessive heat and cold do not follow each other the human race survives in reasonable numbers. And thus everything good, noble or remarkable in any way, in your country or ours, or any country we have heard of, is written down in our temples since time immemorial and thus preserved.'"

The origins of Egyptian history, according to Manetho

But how far back do these "immemorial" times extend?

On this point, opinions differ, as we have seen. Manetho has tried to give us a precise idea using the archives of the Egyptian priests, since he was himself High Priest at the Temple of Heliopolis—considered in the ancient world as a seat of learning. There he had at his disposal a vast quantity of historical material: papyri, hieroglyphic tablets, wall carvings, all sorts of inscriptions and possibly also the expert opinions of colleagues well versed in the age-old traditions of Egypt.

Making use of all these sources, the priest-historian compiled the first history of Ancient Egypt. This work contained, as we have said, a list of the many royal dynasties of Egypt. Unfortunately the work was lost, probably burned during the fire at the Library of Alexandria. Just a few extracts were preserved in the writings of other authors.

Here is one such extract, in which Manetho traced the history of Egypt back to the year 24,920 B.C. "The first man, or god, of Egypt was Hephaistos who was also known as the inventor of fire. His son Helios (the Sun) was succeeded by Sosis, then Cronos, Osiris, Typhon (brother of Osiris) and, finally, Horus, the son of Osiris and Isis. They were the first kings of Egypt. The royal line went from one to the other in uninterrupted succession for a period of 13,900 years. After these gods, the demigods reigned for 1,250 years and there was then a new line of kings for 1,817 years. Then came the thirty kings of Memphis, who established their power for 1,790 years. After this came the reign of the 'Spirits of the Dead' for 5,813 years."

Chapter II

THOUSANDS OF YEARS
BEFORE COPERNICUS AND GALILEO

AMONG the many ruins along the banks of the Nile, there stands at Dendera the temple of Hathor, the goddess of love. In this shrine were practiced the secret rites of Osiris handed down by the faithful since the distant past. On the ceiling of this temple a zodiac was carved which we have already mentioned in connection with Champollion. This remarkable piece of work was removed during the expedition to Egypt, and reconstructed in Paris after having been replaced by a copy. According to Hennig, the signs of this zodiac represent a configuration of stars and planets which can be situated, according to the astrological symbols and with reference to the precession of the equinoxes, at about 5,000 years B.C.

Was the Great Pyramid built in the 34th century B.C.?

Using the Dendera zodiac and the evidence of Herodotus, the English writer Richard Hennig reached the following conclusions: "There is a text of Herodotus (who did not invent things) concerning the events in ancient times upon which the wisdom of the priests was based. This text contains the following passage: 'The Egyptian priests claimed that the Sun rose twice where it sets now and set twice where it rises now.'

"This is the phenomenon known as 'precession of the equinoxes' or the retrograde movement of the equinoctial points. We know that the Earth moves in its orbit on an inclined axis and that this axis, facing a succession of different points, returns to its point of departure every 25,827 years.

"If we take Herodotus literally, we have proof that Egypt knew about astronomy 50,000 years ago. For if the observation of the heavens had not begun at that time, the precession of the equinoxes could not have been calculated. The Greeks discovered the phenomenon in 150 B.C., but the Babylonians had discovered it or had some notion of it long before. They spoke of celestial events which must have happened during the period called the 'Era of Gemini' when this constellation entered the first day of Spring in the solar year.

"We have every reason to believe that the Egyptians had aquired excellent knowledge thanks to long observation of the heavens. The Dendera zodiac (which goes back several centuries before Christ) shows Gemini in the sign of Spring. Logically, and this is the only

At Dendera stood the temple of Hathor, the goddess of Love. It dates back to the ptolemaic era (4th to 1st century B.C.). The mystic cult of Osiris was practiced there. The Zodiac shown here decorated the ceiling of a chapel devoted to this goddess. It shows a constellation of stars and asters, and this 5,000 years before our era! *Musée du Louvre, Giraudon.*

possible conclusion, we must think that Egyptian astronomy goes back at least as far as the 'Era of Gemini' and that the theory that the Great Pyramid was constructed in the 34th century B.C. is quite plausible."

Was the Dendera Zodiac composed by the astronomers of some vanished civilization?

How useful are all these dates? Had the Egyptians really aquired a sophisticated knowledge of astronomy. Does the Dendera zodiac really provide the detailed information that Richard Hennig and many others attribute to it?

Naturally, conventional astronomers give no credence to these theories and declare that primitive peoples, who had no telescopes, had no means of making such observations. Nevertheless it is interesting to mention here certain strange beliefs of the Dogons and other African tribes, studied by Jean Servier, professor of ethnology at Montpellier.

The Dogons are a black race who live on the heights of Bandiagara, in Mali, and who have known for a long time that Sirius has two satellites. The Dogons say that the nearest of these is made of a metal called *sogolu*, which is more brilliant than iron; one grain of this substance weighs as much as 480 "loads" (the load of one donkey). The people of the Sudan worship Sirius as the father of our solar system, confirming the belief of ancient occult science. The Shilluk tribe, in South Africa, has always called Uranus —a planet with two moons—by the name of "Three Stars." But until its discovery by Herschel on March 13, 1781, the planet was unknown to modern astronomy. The Tuaregs share with many other peoples a series of legends concerning Orion and the Pleiades.

Are these simply myths, or can we accept, with C. Daly King, the hypothesis that such a detailed knowledge of the stars, transmitted by generations of primitive peoples for thousands of years, could only have been obtained from the astronomers of some vanished civilization?

A reputable scientist defends the great age of Egyptian civilization

Daly King is convinced that all the extraordinary knowledge of the priests of Thebes and Memphis is the direct legacy of an ancient civilization which disappeared 40,000 years ago.

The man behind this extraordinary theory is not a visionary. He is a scientist well respected by his colleagues for his remarkable psychological research, and the author of three classic text-books which are still in use: *Beyond Behaviourism* (1927), *Integrative Psychology* (1931) and *The Psychology of Consciousness* (1932).

In 1946, Daly King submitted to Yale University a doctoral thesis on the electromagnetic phenomena produced during sleep.

Then he studied the higher states of consciousness, during which we are more awake than normal. This led to another famous book, published in New York in 1963 under the title: *The States of Human Consciousness.* He died that same year while putting the finishing touches to a work devoted to the occult sciences of Ancient Egypt.

The "ankh-en-maat," or mirror of truth

The main argument of Daly King can be summed up thusly: in a remarkably short space of time a decisive event transformed a group of Semitic tribes living beside the Nile into a highly civilized nation which lasted for 3,000 years. This event was, without doubt, the re-discovery of the ancient heritage of a previous Egyptian civilization which flourished on the banks of the Nile 40,000 years ago, before disappearing as the result of a tremendous cataclysm.

The priests who brought about this amazing resurrection of the distant past of Egypt created special schools to preserve for the future this secret knowledge. "In Egypt," wrote Daly King, "there were many schools, and the Great School, which operated within the pyramids, was highly specialized. Its specialty was the objective study of the universe, and one of the courses offered to students was the use of the natural, but hidden functions of the body to transform them from the sub-human state which is that of all of us into full human beings.

"The Great School had perfected a science which is unknown to us: the science of psychological optics. This involved the study of mirrors which reflected only what was evil in any face placed before them. Such a mirror was called the 'ankh-en-maat,' or mirror of truth. Candidates admitted to the Great School could see nothing in the mirror because they had been purified of all evil. Such students were called 'Masters of the Pure Mirror.' "

This thesis has naturally been criticized by conventional Egyptologists: "This theory is based on no evidence and seems completely crazy," wrote one. To which Daly King replied: "If all Egyptologists were boiled and the fluid obtained distilled, one would not extract a microgram of imagination!"

What lies inside the huge artificial caves of Heluan and Sakkara?

The idea of an early Egyptian civilization going back tens of thousands of years, which was wiped out by a catastrophe, is also advanced by a French scholar, Jacques Verne. "The origin of Egyptian civilization," he wrote in the magazine *Constellation*, "does not go back, as Western experts believe, or as they have always written, to almost 40 centuries B.C., but much further.

"More than 10,000 years ago, the Egyptians knew about metals, and had a highly developed knowledge, especially of astronomy. Their calendar was based on the star Sirius, and they already knew that the star has a dark companion which is extremely dense.

"This early civilization was destroyed by a disaster, but enough elements survived to permit the development of the Egypt known to archeologists.

"Everybody knows the classical Egyptian monuments: the Sphinx or the Pyramids, for example. Everyone knows too the archeological discoveries made in Egypt—notably the tombs of the Pharaohs.

But it seems that the Egyptians were always anxious to conceal the most important tombs, especially the huge artificial caves beneath Heluan and Sakkara."

The mysteries of the Egyptian calendar

Indeed it is certain that the finds made in 1954 at Sakkara plunged archeologists into great perplexity.

The Egyptian archeologist Zaki Saad found, among other extraordinary objects, fabrics woven with extremely fine thread on high-precision machinery. "It is difficult to believe," he wrote, "that they were woven on a simple loom. Indeed it seems that weaving was another of the mysteries of the Ancient Egyptians, and we are still groping for a solution." And the Egyptian archeologist also comes to the conclusion that the ancient civilization was technologically far more advanced than we have hitherto supposed.

During the excavations in 1954, mysterious tombs were also found dating from the first dynasty. They were huge—some of them up to 90 feet in length. The Soviet archeologist Garamov, in charge of these operations, claims to have found among these huge tombs mummies, maps of the skies, perfectly spherical crystal lenses, and, above all, inscriptions extending the Egyptian calendar to an incredible date. The inscriptions contained 25 cycles, each of 1,461 years, making a total of 36,525 years.

According to the Soviet archeologist, the lenses found at Sakkara are optical instruments which allowed the Ancient Egyptians to observe the skies, and to establish their strange and mysterious calendar. Garamov pointed out that, already in 1852, the famous English physicist Sir Davis Brewster showed his colleagues during a meeting of the British Association at Bedford a piece of rock crystal fashioned in the shape of a lens, which had just been found in the excavation of Niniveh.

"Sparks of wisdom" and secret knowledge

Such is the great puzzle of Ancient Egyptian astronomy, which has provoked bitter argument between independent researchers and established experts.

Contrary to Garamov, the Soviet author Alexander Kazantsev does not believe that the Egyptians possessed instruments capable of observing the stars. He attributes their observations to "sparks of wisdom," a sort of occult knowledge which allowed them to discover the secrets of the stars and the universe. "Around the pyramids," he wrote, "in the shadow of the columns of the temple of Ra, surrounded by white marble statues of Pallas and Jupiter, or the great emptiness of the desert, the unknown scientists of distant antiquity continually observed the stars and laid the foundations of astronomy. This science of nocturnal calm, solitary contemplation and keen perception, this science of priests, visionaries and navigators, this exact science of time and space, demands instruments of great precision. But in ancient times such instruments did not exist. Given this fact, certain astronomical knowledge of the Ancients cannot fail to amaze us. Thousands of years before Copernicus and Galileo, the Egyptians knew that the Earth was a globe revolving round the Sun. Despite the fact that they had no instruments, they even knew now the Earth rotated. The priests, custodians of this knowledge, had already deduced that the Universe was infinite and full of a multitude of other worlds. We do not understand how the ancients can have known about the elliptical orbit of the Earth around the Sun. Such 'sparks of wisdom' are extremely interesting in their own right. The ancients must have possessed the results of certain calculations, rather than using precise instruments.''

PART SIX

THREE UNSOLVED MYSTERIES

"There is nothing hidden which will not be revealed, and nothing secret which will not be known."

The Gospels

THE three accounts which follow are completely authentic and have been verified by several witnesses.

If their material reality cannot, under any circumstances, be questioned, their significance remains hidden.

We will not try to establish some farfetched connection between them. There is nothing to connect the bleeding hand of a mummy, a voice which seems to come from the 18th dynasty and a naïve painter who can reproduce faithfully, without ever having seen it, a mural from a tomb in the Valley of the Kings.

In the face of such mysteries, we will refrain from idle speculation. Here are these three unusual and disturbing stories.

The "miraculous hand"

At the start of this century, an Alexandrian antique dealer made a strange find. It was a sarcophagus containing the hand of a mummy.

In a short space of time, the rumor spread throughout Alexandria that the hand possessed strange powers.

"You only have to touch it to feel a sensation of warmth," said one witness.

"I saw it bleeding," claimed another.

And since the Orient is fond of magic and miracles, huge crowds flocked to see and touch this amazing hand. The Press got hold of the story of the "bleeding hand" and concocted hundreds of implausible theories to explain it. The occult magazine *Misr*, founded in 1840 by the famous Syrian occultist Ahmed Alassum, devoted a special issue to the hand, to the great delight of the antique dealer, who had the bright idea of charging an entrance fee to those who wished to see and touch the relic. Soon the fame of the "bleeding hand" reached Europe.

The cunning Egyptian sees a profit

One day, a British delegation, led by Sir Frederic Shand, arrived in Alexandria.

The Englishmen had come to acquire the relic, which was rumored to be that of a highborn princess.

The day after their arrival, the delegation went to see the dealer, whose shop was in Cherif-Pacha Street.

"We represent the Westminster Museum," explained Sir Frederic. "We have been told that you possess a strange sarcophagus and the hand of a mummy with strange powers."

"Come in gentlemen," replied the dealer. "But, I warn you, neither the sarcophagus nor the hand is for sale."

"We intend, after examining the hand closely, to offer you a good price."

"The price is immaterial," replied the Egyptian. "I repeat that I intend to keep them."

The antique dealer, who saw a handsome profit, thought it better not to give in straight away.

Day after day, the delegation returned to negotiate. The cunning Egyptian bargained with his visitors, but would not give them a definite answer, hoping that the Englishmen would gradually increase their offer.

The mysterious sarcophagus

And indeed it seemed that Sir Frederic and his companions were more and more interested in these relics.

During their many visits, they discovered that the sarcophagus too possessed strange powers, not unlike those of the hand. They noticed that, by placing their hands on the face and chest of this mummiform sarcophagus, they felt, less than one minute later, a strange sensation of warmth.

In addition to this, their bodies experienced a tingling sensation which became gradually more intense. This effect was so powerful that one member of the delegation passed out after having kept his hand for too long on the sarcophagus.

More and more intrigued, the Enlish team urged the dealer to make up his mind.

"You will never be offered such a good price," declared Sir Frederic. "You are losing an opportunity of making your fortune."

"Perhaps," replied the Egyptian, "but I will make more by keeping the relics, which earn me money every day."

After several weeks of bargaining, the delegation tried one last approach. But the dealer refused categorically to give up the precious objects.

All trace of the relics is lost in Hollywood

The Arab was not mistaken.

As months went by, huge crowds continued to gather in front of the shop, which had become a place of pilgrimage.

The crowds were so huge that the police were often called in to clear the road and let the trafic pass.

And the walls around the sarcophagus were soon covered with messages of gratitude.

Some claimed to have won money, others to have recovered from an incurable disease, thanks to the miraculous hand. People kissed it and embraced it. They told it of their hopes and fears.

When World War I broke out, the many soldiers passing through

Alexandria went to see the mummy to place themselves under its protection. Certain members of the Australian Expeditionary Force, who survived the deadly landing attempt near Gallipoli, claimed that they were still alive thanks to the "miraculous hand."

Between the wars, the sarcophagus was shipped to the United States, where it was to be exhibited in various cities.

After many months on tour, it reached Hollywood, and there all trace of it is lost.

Perhaps it is still in the property room of a movie studio...

English nuns and xenoglotism

The second story is equally true and equally incredible. Before telling it, however, we must explain the term "xenoglotism," since it is involved in the strange adventure of a young English girl we shall call Rosemary.

Composed of two Greek words "foreign" and "tongue," xenoglotism offers one of the strangest examples of parapsychology.

It is the ability of a subject to speak, while in a state of trance, in a foreign tongue of which he has no knowledge whatsoever. There are two documented examples of this extremely rare phenomenon.

In 1634, the nuns of the Convent of Ursulines in London began to talk, in a collective state of trance, in Greek, Latin, Turkish and Spanish, although they had no knowledge of these languages. And, in the middle of the last century, the American Laura Edwards, pronounced in a trance many phrases in Ancient Greek, a language she had never studied.

A common love of death

The story of Rosemary is even more incredible.

It begins in December, 1927. A schoolteacher in Blackpool, Rosemary met Dr. Frederic Herbert Wood, who taught music at the same school. And since the evenings in Blackpool were rather dull, Rosemary used to visit Dr. Wood, whose love of music she shared.

Dr. Wood's hobby was parapsychology, but the subject did not interest Rosemary, and he did not say much to her about his research.

On December 13, 1927, Rosemary went, as usual, to her friend's house. She sat down at a table and began to draw strange symbols on a sheet of paper. Intrigued by this, Dr. Wood asked her the meaning of these signs, which looked, at first sight, like hieroglyphics. But Rosemary was unable to explain their meaning. She intimated, however, that she had been guided "by a strange, unknown power."

Strange sounds from the distant past

During the days that followed, Dr. Wood, who realized that Rosemary was a "true medium," asked her to repeat the experiment. She drew more hieroglyphic characters.

To find out more about this, Dr. Wood showed these strange drawings to the famous Egyptologist Alfred J. Howard Hulme, an Oxford Professor. He confirmed that they were genuine Egyptian hieroglyphics, correctly drawn and with a precise meaning. Intrigued

Auguste Lesage, was the greatest "painter-medium of Europe." When visiting Egypt in 1939, he found on the wall of a small tomb in the Valley of the Kings, a big fresco which was a replica of his painting "The Harvest" which he had painted before leaving for Egypt. *Roger-Viollet*.

by this phenomenon, Wood continued to keep a close eye on Rosemary's strange gift for several years.

Suddenly, on August 8, 1931, Rosemary started to utter strange words which seemed to belong to no known language. Could it be Ancient Egyptian? Wood consulted Professor Hulme again. The latter traveled to Blackpool to witness this incredible phenomenon for himself. At his request, Rosemary "spoke." The sounds were confused at first, but slowly became clearer: "Ah-yita-zhula." The professor managed to decipher these strange sounds, which meant in Ancient Egyptian: "I have heard someone speaking."

At whose dictation was Rosemary speaking? Who was the "someone"? For several months the medium continued to utter strange sounds originating from the distant past. "I can sense the words I am saying," explained Rosemary, "like a sort of inaudible language. They are formed in a different part of the brain than normal language. I have a feeling that it lies somewhere between the brain and the top of the skull.

"When a person speaks, he usually thinks first. But when the voice is there, my mind is a blank. My lips move and form words; but I cannot say how. Usually we remember what we have said, at least for a moment or so; but I can recall nothing of what I may have said in a state of trance. I am unable to repeat these words or remember their meaning."

Was Telika the wife of Amenhotep III?

On December 5, 1931, in the presence of Dr. Wood, Professor Hulme and other eminent specialists in Egyptian history, Rosemary pronounced twenty-eight phrases in Ancient Egyptian. Hulme managed to decipher all of them, and learned that the "voice" dictating to Rosemary was that of Telika—a Babylonian princess who had gone to Egypt during the reign of Amenhotep III.

Who was she? We can only surmise. Was she a wife of Amenhotep III? It is quite possible. The Amarna tablets provide us with some interesting information. For example, the Pharaoh Amenhotep III married the sister of the Babylonian King Kadashman. Was this Telika? In the correspondence exchanged by the Pharaoh and the King, the latter expresses his surprise at Amenhotep's desire to marry his daughter. "Why," he asks, "does the Pharaoh wish to marry my daughter when he is already married to my sister? And what has become of that sister?"

Such are the questions of Kadashman to Amenhotep, and in a letter found at Amarna in 1887, he writes: "No one has seen my sister... and no one knows if she is alive or dead. The Pharaoh has said to my envoys, when presenting his wives to them, 'Behold, there is your princess, standing before you.' But my envoys did not recognize her. Is this woman really my sister?"

The occult powers of the High Priests

What exactly did happen? Was Telika murdered as the result of one of the many harem intrigues? Did Queen Teje, the principal wife of Amenhotep III, "liquidate" her rival?

In a study devoted to the medium Rosemary, Professor Hulme leads us to believe so. He connects these events to the first signs of the Atonist heresy, later to become for a short time the state religion of Egypt, on the accession of Ikhnaton.

Telika would have been a secret convert to the rising cult of Aton, and would have tried to influence her husband to make it law. This would explain why the principal wife, hostile to the new religion and in league with the priests of Amon, would have had her rival murdered.

The words of Telika, through the mouth of Rosemary, seem to confirm Hulme's hypothesis. "I know that the great power of the priests is founded on superstition, which allows them to dominate and subjugate the people, who are afraid of them...

"The priests of the highest rank used the occult sciences, such as telepathy. They could predict their own future. Much of their learning has never been written down, and only the priests of the very highest rank knew about such things."

A beam of blue light from another world

From April 1936, Dr. Wood and Professor Hulme, assisted by Dr. Nandor Fodor of the Institute of Psychical Research, started to record the speech of Rosemary on disk. Several English and foreign Egyptologists joined forces to decipher these messages from the distant past.

Through the lips of Rosemary, Telika, the murdered princess, revealed certain secrets about Ancient Egypt. On the construction of the Pyramids, she confirmed that the builders of these monuments had developed sophisticated lifting devices based on precise mechanical calculations. They could produce electricity from the air, and used a form of lighting "the effects of which are similar to those of modern illumination." Egyptian sages also possessed, according to Telika, "knowledge which would be of incalculable value to the modern world if it could be re-discovered."

In a recording made of May 4, 1936, Telika, through Rosemary, made this astonishing declaration: "I would like to tell you something about the superior forms of life here in the other world. It is hard to describe them. We have learned strange things from these beings; but it is just as difficult for me to make contact with them as it is with you. Yet a dead soul may approach them more easily than it may approach you on Earth. Your system of values is incomplete. The planet Earth is so little developed compared with most of the others. Human knowledge and progress are at a low level compared to those of these superior beings. Your civilization is like a drop of water in a vast ocean. We are not much more developed ourselves. You speak of our faculties and powers, but I am nothing and know next to nothing. Sometimes when I am in the state which you call meditation, I feel that my body is pierced by a beam of blue light from another world. It is a source of beauty, strength and awareness. Those who protect me here say that these are the rays of a higher consciousness into which I will merge when I have lost contact with all things on Earth. With their limited intelligence, humans cannot tolerate the idea that they will never be able to comprehend the limitless power of the Universe."

Rosemary heaved a deep sigh, and began to speak in Ancient Egyptian

The last recording made by Wood, Hulme and Fodor dates from May 30, 1936. Dr. Wood has described the circumstances of this last "séance," which was witnessed by many Egyptologists, scholars and psychologists.

Rosemary sat down in a small room and was given several sheets of paper, in case she needed to write. Then the recording engineers set up their equipment in an adjoining room. "A few moments later," wrote Dr. Wood, "Rosemary heaved a deep sigh—this can be heard at the start of the recording—and began to speak in Ancient Egyptian, in slow disjointed phrases. I numbered these phrases in the sequence in which they occur on the recording, including the pauses. Sometimes the sense is clear, at other times the end of one phrase merges into the beginning of the next, or even a later phrase."

The moving words of Telika

The last recording session was to be a sort of test conducted by Professor Gunn.

Gunn, who lectured in Egyptology at Oxford, had questioned this psychic experiment. He believed that Rosemary was not speaking Ancient Egyptian. Asked by Dr. Wood to answer her critic, here is what Rosemary-Telika said during the "séance."

The words were decoded and translated by a team of Egyptologists, and professor Gunn was forced to admit his error. The language was undoubtedly Ancient Egyptian.

Here is the text of this statement, a statement full of pathetic pauses, where Telika, in a desperate attempt to convince her detractor, calls us to her aid and asks us to bear witness to her sincerity.

"We have come to record... what is said. It is a test... to satisfy the ear. It will show... and prove... there is really a message... Indeed... this has already been done... by a metal object (the recording machine)... It was done to make easy... the difficult task... to make clear what was said... It has not yet been necessary... That is how it is... It is just as I have said... This power permits... But it is lost... Help me... finish the phrase!... Those who live in the spirit world... to the extent that they have perceived what the ear cannot hear... give me the chance... of improving that... When you see that, we come... and tell of our disappointment... When you see that you must put an end to this misunderstanding; I make this... statement... So think... Agree and approve... and support what has been written ... this time ... All this is designed to ... overcome opposition. Show your approval ... bear witness to it ... bear witness to it ... bear witness to it ... Help me ... Make a declaration which commits you ... Forget what has been said ... Have done with it ... Give your hand ... It must destroy ... the weak points and prevent ... any more explanations ... Let him listen to this ... it will show what has happened."

A voice from the 18th dynasty

Such is the astonishing story of Rosemary, the Blackpool schoolteacher who acted as interpreter to a Babylonian princess murdered 3,000 years ago.

Today, most of those who took part in this psychic experiment have disappeared. Rosemary died in 1961, Dr. Wood and professor Hulme in 1967, and the repentant critic, professor Gunn, in 1969.

However, we are left with one piece of concrete evidence of this unique experiment: the records themselves, preserved in London, for students of parapsychology and Ancient Egypt to hear when they choose that voice from the 18th dynasty.

Augustin Lesage—the greatest painter-medium in Europe

Does this mean that certain ancient Egyptians continue to live among us?

Such is the belief of the famous Austrian occultist Karl Eisner, who is convinced that the occult science of Egypt has allowed certain initiates from the days of the Pharaohs to conquer death. These would be the "living-dead," who sometimes manifest themselves in strange ways. Eisner urges us to be vigilant and listen carefully to these "voices of eternal Egypt."

If this is so, is the artisan Mena, who lived in the reign of Rameses II, one of these "living-dead?" The story of Augustin Lesage—our third example—offers some proof of this.

Nothing predestined Lesage to become one day the greatest painter-medium in Europe, and thereby associate his name with the incredible story of Rosemary. From a poor family of miners in northern France, Augustin Lesage went down the mine in his turn in 1909, at the age of fourteen.

One day in 1911, while he was working alone at the coalface, he heard a strange voice coming out of nowhere. Startled, the young miner stopped digging and listened carefully. After a moment, the voice was heard again. "One day, Augustin, you will be an artist!"

Convinced that this was some sort of hallucination, Lesage shrugged his shoulders and carried on working. Him, an artist? He didn't know anything about painting . . .

Does the key to the mystery lie in Egypt?

Nevertheless, some time after this strange episode, Augustin realized that he was changing. He felt a genuine desire to paint, and soon began to make sketches. Then he bought canvases and paints. All his pictures had an Egyptian theme.

Painting was like second nature to him. An unknown hand seemed to guide him, dictating even the smallest details. His canvases were authentic frescoes from the time of the Pharaohs, although he had never been to Egypt.

His family witnessed this strange transformation in astonishment. His pictures were so remarkable that people from Lille, Roubaix and Tourcoing were eager to buy them. The fame of this miner-artist soon spread beyond the North of France. Parisian galleries bought up his pictures.

But why did they all depict Egyptian scenes? Why was his source of inspiration a country he had no knowledge of? What was the unknown hand that guided him? Lesage could not answer these questions, but he decided to travel to Egypt, hoping that he might find there the key to the mystery.

The strange "Harvest" of Augustin Lesage

On February 20, 1939, Lesage set off from Marseille on board the ship *El Mansour* for Egypt.

He traveled with a group of tourists organized by the *Association Guillaume Bude*, an association of classical scholars. Several French archeologists were there to act as guides and inform the tourists about the history and meaning of the Egyptian remains.

During the crossing, Lesage struck up an aquaintance with an eminent Egyptologist, to whom he showed a dozen of his pictures. One of them was called "The Harvest."

"You seem particularly proud of that one," said the archeologist.

"Yes," said Lesage, "that's my latest work. I have been told that there is in a recently discovered tomb a fresco like my painting. This seems incredible and I am dying to see it."

"That's amazing," answered the scholar, who thought that he was dealing with a madman.

"What I felt ... went beyond mere curiosity"

The boat arrived at Alexandria on February 26, 1939. On the first day Lesage visited several monuments: the statue of Rameses III, the sphinx at Memphis, the pyramid of Sakkara, the pyramids of Cheops, Chephren and Mycerinus, and lastly, the great Sphinx of Gizeh.

This is what he wrote later about his first trip: "I think that tourists are in general very interested in these monuments, huge statues, relics of the grandeur and beauty of a civilization which lasted several thousands of years. I must say that for my part I felt a powerful sensation going beyond mere curiosity, as if the stones were familiar, as if this new country which I had never seen was not completely unknown, and I felt attachment rather than admiration."

An undefinable bond

On the following days, Lesage visited the Cairo Museum. On March 4, he went south, to Upper Egypt.

Aswan, Edfu, Luxor, Karnak were the main stopping points. Then the group came to the Valley of the Kings.

When they reached a small village which had been excavated two years earlier, the guide explained that in the reign of Rameses II the place had been inhabited by hundreds of workmen connected with burials.

One of them, called Mena, had obtained permission to build for himself in his spare time a tomb just beyond the village.

"We visited this small tomb, which contained about twenty coffins, and suddenly I saw on the wall a huge fresco. I recognized the harvest scene which I had painted just before leaving. I was strangely disturbed by this and find it difficult to describe my emotions.

"Standing so close to this picture and seeing how similar it was to the one I had painted, it seemed as if I were the artist. There was an undefinable bond between the painting and myself. I could not tell if I had painted it or had just discovered it. I stood there motionless, elated and overwhelmed by surprise and delight. I was filled with immense joy, like an exile returning home."

"My hand is the instrument of a brain which is not mine"

One of his friends who was with him, as well as other tourists who had seen the painting, shared his amazement. The two were amazingly similar. The fresco was in a tomb——one that was little known and infrequently visited——and it had never been reproduced.

What was the explanation? Had the spirit of Mena guided the hand of the painter-medium?

"I understood at last," wrote Lesage, "why I had not made this journey to Egypt earlier. It was important that I should not visit Egypt before the discovery of this fresco; I had to see it and prove that my paintings are not the products of my own imagination, but that my hand is the instrument of a brain that is not my own."

For several years, a large number of occultists and parapsychologists questioned Lesage about his strange gift. But to all these questions he modestly replied: "I don't know. It's an unknown hand which guides my own." On February 21, 1954, the painter-medium died in the village of Burbure in the Pas-de-Calais (northern France), carrying his secret with him.

Occultists: visionaries, or pioneers of a new knowledge?

What can we conclude from these three accounts? Should we follow Karl Eisner in believing that the Ancient Egyptians still live among us?

One fact is certain: modern science has no explanation for these strange phenomena, which remain the closed domain of spiritualist circles and parapsychologists. The curse of the Pharaohs is part of this secret domain, bequeathed by scientists to amateurs——who are legion——of the unusual, the inexplicable and the unknown.

However, certain scientists are uneasy about this and wonder if they have the right to treat with contempt all those who venture into the domain of the unknown. Are they merely visionaries who, having failed to find God, are chasing false beliefs and inventing ghostly idols to fill the heavens, and who lack true faith? Or are they the pioneers of a new knowledge as yet undefined by science? Henri Poincaré, the great French mathematician, seems to have believed that the second term of this alternative was the right one. "As regards the relationship of modern science with the unknown," he confided to his friend Cocteau, "I should say that we are just hearing the first knockings at the doors."

Montaigne held that it was "a stupid presumption to disdain as false what seems improbable to us, which is a common fault among those who claim to have some measure of common sense.

"I used to do the same, and if I heard tell of ghosts or fortune-telling, spells and witchcraft, or some other story beyond my comprehension, I felt sorry for the poor people who were taken in by such superstition.

"And now I find that I was as much to be pitied myself."

But it is also true that Montaigne, a descendant of Spanish Jews[1], who often were *Alumbrados*, was connected through them with ancient occult science.

We will leave the reader to make up his own mind...

---

1.   See: Roger Trinquet, *Montaigne's Youth*, 1972.

Printed in Spain
Published by Ferni
Distributed by Friends of History

Imprenta Sevillana, S.A., Dos Hermanas (Sevilla),
Km. 553, Carretera Madrid-Cádiz
Depósito Legal SE 629 - 1977. Tomo 2